CONQUER
ANXIETY
WORKBOOK
FOR TEENS

CONQUER ANXIETY WORKBOOK FOR TEENS

Find Peace from Worry, Panic, Fear, and Phobias

BY TABATHA CHANSARD, PhD

Illustrations by Fotini Tikkou

ALTHEA
PRESS

For Matthieu and Geneviève, with unconditional love.

A humble thank you to all my patients and their families for allowing me to be a part of your journey toward inner peace. Each and every one of you has taught me something from your unique perspective. Working with you has made me into a stronger therapist and allowed me to better help others.

Interior and Cover Designer: Suzanne LaGasa
Art Producer: Sara Feinstein
Editor: Melissa Valentine
Production Editor: Andrew Yackira
Illustrations © 2019 Fotini Tikkou

ISBN: Print 978-1-64152-401-8 | eBook 978-1-64152-402-5

CONTENTS

Part 2

Calming Your Anxious Mind 25

Part 3

Calming Your Anxious Body 65

Part 4

Putting Your Tools to Work Q&A 99

INTRODUCTION

Living with anxiety is such a burden. It can feel like your flaws are constantly exposed to the world. Perhaps you try to be perfect to convince others and even yourself that you've got it all together, while inside you feel like a mess, always on edge, always about to break from the weight of the unease. You can feel enormous, overwhelming, and lonely pressure.

Anxiety can also be a really difficult emotion to manage. After all, the world has so many stressors. Add to that everything you have to deal with as a teen. I get it. I wrote this book because I want you to know that you are not alone, that anxiety is a normal emotion, and that you have the power and ability to deal with it.

I've had the honor of working with many teens who felt that anxiety ruled their lives. As a therapist who treats anxious teens, I've also celebrated their successes as they overcame this burden. With some guidance and practice using healthy coping skills, you too can break free from your constant doubts about yourself. You can harness that anxious energy into momentum that helps you strive toward your goals and achieve them with confidence.

We'll begin by examining the different ways anxiety can affect your life. I will also help you identify what kinds of anxiety you may be experiencing.

Next, I will empower you with tools and tricks you can use. You'll learn the two main ways for attacking anxiety: (1) through your thoughts and (2) through your body. I'll explain how anxiety plays tricks on your thinking and how you can think more realistically. Then I'll show you some ways you can release anxiety from your physical body and stand up to anxiety through your actions.

Finally, we'll explore several real-life scenarios that show different ways anxiety manifests in life, how it can affect you, and how you can put these tools to work to defeat anxiety and increase your confidence.

While the exercises in this book may seem simple, in reality, hard work is required to make changes and use new skills every day. You will need time, dedication, and repetition to break old habits for dealing with anxiety and to learn new ones. So please be patient with yourself as you work through the book. The process will not be perfect. You will encounter speed bumps along the way. But if you stick with it, ask for help when you need it, and keep encouraging yourself, you will get better and better at it. You have taken the first step by picking up this book, so read on to learn more about which anxiety traits you can relate to, what causes them, and how you can overcome them for good!

Part One

THE TRUTH ABOUT ANXIETY

You probably know the feelings: You're tense, your heart is beating faster, your mind is racing with all the things that could possibly go wrong, you're doubting yourself, you're fearing the worst, your gut is doing somersaults, and blood is rushing to your face. Too much to deal with! But this is how many teens feel when they experience anxiety. Anxiety can come on quickly and overwhelm you before you even know what hit you. It can be absolutely miserable, and surely anyone who experiences it would want to get rid of it from their life completely, right? But there's something you should know. In reality, we *need* anxiety. Anxiety can actually help us, when it is kept in check.

Anxiety Is Trying to Help (Even If It Doesn't Feel That Way)

Think about when you wash your hands, or when you look both ways before crossing the street, or when you check over your answers before turning in your test. Believe it or not, these everyday actions come from a place of mild anxiety, which helps you stay free from illness, safe from danger, and capable of doing your best work. Without a little anxiety, you would be too careless and prone to risky behavior. However, anxiety can become a problem when it grows beyond its helpful and protective function. When it gets out of hand, anxiety can cause problems rather than help you solve them. Anxiety has become too much when . . .

* it interferes with your life.

* you struggle to find calm and peace from day to day.

* your brain cannot tell the difference between fearful situations in real life and fearful situations you created with your thoughts alone.

What can cause your anxiety to become "too much"? Unfortunately, no one knows for certain what makes some people feel anxiety more intensely than others. But researchers have found that this type of anxiety is likely due to heredity, along with the individual's environment and experiences. Let's explore how this happens:

Heredity: Years of research have shown us that anxiety is in our genes. That means you may be more likely to experience some kind of anxiety if your parents or grandparents have anxiety. But genetics doesn't always determine how you experience anxiety. For example, your mother may be a worrier and generally anxious about almost everything, but your sister may have anxiety only about heights, so much so that she can't ride elevators higher than the second floor. You, on the other hand, might have test anxiety and struggle during exams. Even though you all have similar genetics, each person's anxiety can look different.

Environment and experiences: Anxiety may also be influenced by our experiences and interactions with others. Perhaps people in your life have reacted to difficult situations with a lot of anxiety, so without you knowing it, you were taught that anxiety is the way to deal with challenges. This "lesson" may have happened repeatedly throughout your life, or even just once. You may be able to remember a significant situation in which this happened, or the experience may have been so subtle that you have no memory of it. Regardless, we do know that the world around us influences what we believe about ourselves and how to approach problems and challenges.

When Anxiety Hangs on Too Long

Let's say something really negative happened to you, like being bullied in middle school. Maybe you dealt with that situation by avoiding the bullies, keeping to yourself, and worrying about potential interactions with these people. This anxious response likely kept you safe, or at least reduced the amount of bullying you experienced from day to day. Through this experience, you learned that an anxious response was helpful. But fast-forward to today, when let's say you are no longer experiencing bullying, and you have a positive group of friends. But you are still living your life with anxiety and responding to challenges with fear and avoidance. Why? Because you learned to react that way in the past. However, now that behavior is actually not helping you. Now it is keeping you from confidently hanging out with your friends or meeting new peers, and it stops you from participating in activities that you would probably enjoy. What used to help you now stops you from really being yourself. This is an example of how not all lessons learned continue to be helpful!

You're Definitely Not Alone

Anxiety is a common emotion that many teens struggle with. Problematic anxiety is experienced by almost one-third (32 percent) of teenagers between the ages of 13 and 18. This means that one out of every three teens is likely to have high levels of anxiety. That's a lot! It also means that you are not alone, even if you feel like you are the only one who feels this way. Even though people may not talk openly about their anxiety, that does not mean they have not felt it. They may deal with anxiety every day.

Let's look at social media, for example. Why does everyone look so happy? On social media we typically see only the happy, carefree experiences of our peers—because that is how people choose to present themselves and the way they want others to see them. We don't see the anxiety and struggles that so many of our friends are experiencing in between their posts. This makes us feel alone in our anxiety, as though no one else could possibly understand.

While anxiety is a challenging emotion and everyone feels anxiety differently, chances are at least one person you know can totally relate to what you are going through. You might be very surprised by who it is. Talking more openly about anxiety can help us feel less alone and find people to support us as we work to take control of this emotion.

Anxiety: A Balancing Act

As you read through this book, always remember that a certain amount of anxiety is helpful and keeps us alert. Therefore, learning to control anxiety to keep it at a manageable level—not to eliminate it completely—is the balancing act you'll want to achieve.

In this book you will learn about three main areas to deal with anxiety: relaxing your physical body, changing your thoughts, and facing fears with brave behaviors. Strategies in these three areas can help diminish the main types of anxiety teens experience:

* General anxiety

* Social anxiety

* Specific fears/phobias

* Panic attacks/panic disorder

You may have experienced one or several of these types of anxiety in your life. In this section you will learn about each of these types of anxiety and identify if you may be experiencing one or more of them. Later in the book, you will learn how to cope with your anxiety in the healthiest ways possible.

General Anxiety

Have you ever bombarded yourself with questions like these?

"What if I fail the test?"

"What if I don't finish my homework in time?"

"What if I don't make the team?"

"What if my voice trembles when I give my speech?"

"What if I say something stupid in front of my crush?"

"What if I don't get invited to the party?"

"What if they laugh at me?"

"What if I embarrass myself?"

"What if I make a mistake and everyone sees me mess up?"

"What if my parents are disappointed in me?"

"WHAT IF?!"

Do you doubt outcomes and yourself all day? If so, you probably don't think about the *most likely* outcomes to these questions. Your mind fixates on the worst thing that could happen, an outcome that is always some form of complete disaster or catastrophe. "If I fail the test, everyone will be disappointed in me. I'll fail the class. My GPA will drop. I won't get into the colleges I want. My parents will be so disappointed in me. I'll never get a job. I'll be a complete failure!" This type of black-and-white, disastrous thinking is at the heart of unhelpful anxiety—it sucks up all your energy and makes you feel like you can't cope or problem-solve. Later in this book, we will explore how you can think differently, believe in your abilities, and act with confidence so you can manage the problems you face.

General anxiety gets its name because the anxiety experienced can be about anything—school, work, relationships with parents, teachers, friends, classmates, extracurricular activities, your safety, your health, and so forth. You worry almost constantly as your brain begins to think that everything must be met with worry and distress. Some people think that this amount of worry helps them get things accomplished or stay safe, but, in reality, it typically has the opposite effect, keeping you from doing your best or engaging in fun activities, and it can cause you to have problems socially.

Still, I understand that you might worry a lot. Experiencing anxiety during adolescence is especially challenging because you're going through so many changes in your life. You are constantly faced with new experiences and have unique pressures to deal with:

* Your brain and body are constantly changing and growing.

* You are gaining more freedom and independence to do things without your parents.

* You have more complex social relationships—you may have begun dating and dealing with romantic relationship issues.

* You are figuring out who you are and what you may want to do with your life as adulthood gets closer.

* You have academic pressures and thoughts about future education and occupations.

* You have so many adults in your life who have expectations of you—including teachers, principals, coaches/instructors, leaders, parents, and friends' parents.

* You are trying to figure out what you believe in, whom to trust, and what to expect from a lot of new experiences, and these things are always changing.

All this can add up to fear and uncertainty, so it makes sense that you have extra anxiety and worry. But all these changes and decisions you have to make are normal—every teenager has had to do this, and the uncertainty doesn't have to own you. In this book you will learn how you can get through this time with less anxiety and more confidence!

Symptoms Checklist: General Anxiety

General anxiety looks a little different for each person, but here are some of the most common symptoms. Do any of these apply to you? If so, check the ones that do:

☐ I feel worried or anxious more often than I feel calm or relaxed.

☐ I worry so much that it feels out of control.

☐ Worry affects my performance at school, my activities, and/or my relationships with friends or family.

I feel one or more of the following:

☐ Restless and on edge

☐ Irritable and easily annoyed

☐ Tired and less energetic

☐ Difficulty concentrating

☐ Tense muscles

☐ Stomach pain and/or nausea

☐ Headaches

☐ Difficulty falling or staying asleep

If you checked four or more of the boxes, good for you for reading this book! Keep reading—you're going to learn some awesome tools for dealing with anxiety in new ways.

Austin's Self-Fulfilling Prophecy

Austin is 15 and a sophomore in high school. He's taking five advanced placement classes and puts all his efforts toward making good grades and having a high GPA, with a goal of attending the university from which both of his parents graduated. He sees how smart and successful his parents and two older siblings are. Even though his parents tell him to "just do his best," he feels that if he doesn't follow in their footsteps, he is failing, and they will all be disappointed in him. He feels a lot of pressure and constantly worries that he isn't doing what it takes to succeed.

Austin spends every waking hour focused on school. He comes home and immediately starts studying and doing homework. He often thinks that his work isn't good enough and that his teachers will fail him. Nights before exams are the worst. He studies until three or four o'clock in the morning, and even then he worries he will fail. He is often tired, on edge, and so focused on schoolwork that he won't even consider going out with his friends on the weekends. His parents encourage him to take breaks and not to worry about grades, but he just can't stop working.

While he obsesses about doing his best, he actually finds it hard to concentrate during class and while studying. His mind wanders as he thinks about what would happen if he failed or what his teachers would think about him. He thinks about how much work he has to do and feels like he just can't keep up. His fatigue and distraction cause Austin to make errors on his homework, quizzes, and tests, even when he is fully prepared and knows the material. It's so frustrating—he tries so hard! Of course, his grades start to suffer, and that makes him even more anxious. As he becomes more anxious, he has more sleepless nights and more distracting thoughts, and even physical symptoms. During quizzes and tests, his heart races, his face flushes, and his body shakes. His mind starts to go blank during class, and he can only think about how he is a failure and will never get into college.

What has gone wrong? How could a dedicated student like Austin struggle so much? Are Austin's thoughts about failure actually causing him to fail?

This vicious cycle is common with anxiety and is called a self-fulfilling prophecy. This means that the very outcome that was feared does happen—not because Austin isn't smart or not capable but because the fear changed the way he thinks and acts. The anxiety becomes a problem, paralyzing him with fear, rather than helping him do his best.

What do you think would have happened if instead of anxious thoughts, Austin had thoughts of confidence? If anxiety was not overwhelming Austin, do you think he would have had such struggles with his coursework? Even if Austin didn't do all of his work perfectly, he earned his way into those advanced placement classes. Do you think he is still capable of making good grades and getting into the college of his choice? Why do you think Austin doesn't believe in himself?

Social Anxiety

Almost every teenager wakes up and goes to school wondering what others are going to think of them. "Will anyone notice the pimple on my nose?" "What will people think of my outfit?" "Is Alex going to notice me today?" "Where will I sit at lunch?" "I hope the teacher doesn't call on me to answer questions." This self-doubt is so common, and, seriously, it happens to almost everyone—even adults! But it happens more in adolescence. This experience of feeling like everyone is focused on you is called the "imaginary audience." Read on to learn about this phenomenon.

The Imaginary Audience

Do you feel like everyone is watching you? The imaginary audience is something many teens feel, and it usually starts in middle school. It makes you feel like you are the center of attention, that everyone sees your every move. Sometimes this makes you feel special and important, but more often it makes you feel worried and self-conscious. The good news is that this feeling of being on stage generally goes away as you get older and feel more confident in yourself.

Social anxiety is similar to the imaginary audience experience, but social anxiety tends to be more intense and more difficult to deal with. If you have social anxiety, you think about others judging you and possibly rejecting you almost constantly. You worry that you will be negatively judged for even the slightest things, like bringing your lunch instead of ordering from the cafeteria, or having a blemish, or saying *hi* to someone new. Simple daily social tasks can become overwhelming and cause you to shrink away from anything social, as you hope not to be noticed at all.

If you feel this way, try to remember this: While it's true that teens observe one another and compare themselves to one another, teens are typically more concerned with how they themselves are being perceived. So basically everyone is so preoccupied with themselves that they aren't likely to be spending too much time judging you!

Avoiding . . . Everything

If you experience social anxiety, you probably don't want to participate in activities that might draw attention to you. You may avoid things like extracurricular activities, social clubs, dances, public speaking, and sleepovers. Going to school and even just hanging out with your friends may be too much to handle. You may not be able to approach your teachers when you have a question. You might get extremely nervous when the hallways are crowded or when you have to find a place to sit during an assembly. You believe that everyone is focused on you and eager to find flaws in everything you do. And once they find those flaws, you're sure they will reject you or humiliate you. But is any of this true? Is it realistic?

What's the big deal, anyway? What's wrong with keeping to yourself? Well, avoidance only makes these feelings worse. Through avoidance, you may not experience as much anxiety in the short term, but this way of living leads to more anxiety and social problems in the long term. Avoidance keeps you from having positive social experiences that can disprove to your brain that everyone dislikes you. Avoidance prevents you from having fun experiences. Avoidance also delays learning how to engage socially, a skill you will need throughout your life.

As you can see, learning about how to overcome social anxiety is worth the effort. As you do, this will lead you to be more confident and open to positive social experiences.

Symptoms Checklist: Social Anxiety

Just about every teenager experiences some degree of social worries, but the following symptoms are indicators of significant social anxiety. Do any of these apply to you? Check the ones you can relate to:

☐ Significant fear of being judged or scrutinized by my peers and/or adults

☐ Fear that I will embarrass myself

☐ Fear that my anxiety will be seen and negatively judged by others

☐ Fear that I will be rejected by my peers or even adults

☐ Avoidance of social situations or intense fear and/or distress in social situations

☐ Fear of social situations that prevents me from doing things I would otherwise enjoy (for example, part of me wants to go to the football game, but my fear of peers negatively judging me keeps me at home)

Even if you checked just one of these boxes, you could benefit from some of the skills discussed in this book. It never hurts to learn ways to feel more confident in your social activities!

Hayley's Humiliation

Hayley is 14 and just started her freshman year in high school. She tends to be quiet and has a couple of great friends, but they aren't going to the same school that she's attending this year. Hayley is terrified to meet new people and make new friends. She feels so alone and has stomachaches every day during the first week of school. She walks the halls with her arms crossed and her head down, hoping no one notices her clothes or makes fun of her hair. During lunch, she pretends to have extra homework so she can eat alone in the library and avoid the embarrassment of asking her peers if she can sit with them—which would be humiliating!

During math, she knows the answers to the questions the teacher asks, but she doesn't speak up. She doesn't want anyone to think that she is a show-off or a teacher's pet. When she sees one of the "popular girls" smirk in her direction, she immediately assumes the girl and her friends are making fun of her. They must think she is completely gross. She starts to feel nauseated and hot, so she goes to the nurse and asks to go home. The next day, she begs her mother to let her stay home from school, because she cannot handle these feelings anymore!

What do you think Hayley is experiencing? Have you ever felt this way before? Is Hayley overanalyzing? Is Hayley's prediction that the popular girls are making fun of her realistic? Could there be other explanations for the "popular girl's" smirk? Do you think avoiding interactions and school is helpful? Why might avoidance make her anxiety worse?

Specific Fears/Phobias

When you think of *phobias*, you may think of all those long, weird-sounding words that describe different fears. Some sound a little bizarre, like koumpounophobia (the fear of buttons) or numerophobia (the fear of numbers; maybe you can use this to get out of doing your math homework!). While these rare fears are fun to think about, the reality of having a true phobia is far from fun and can make life really difficult. Anyone can have an excessive fear of anything, but there are common phobias that adolescents often experience, including these:

* Fear of throwing up or being sick in public (emetophobia)

* Fear of being enclosed in small spaces (claustrophobia)

* Fear of heights (acrophobia)

* Fear of spiders, snakes, or insects (arachnophobia, ophidiophobia, or entomophobia)

* Fear of needles/injections (aichmophobia)

* Fear of flying (aerophobia)

Sure, most people don't like spiders and snakes and have some fear of being around them, but what makes a fear a phobia is when that fear is so intense that it stops you from living your life normally. For example, someone with a phobia of spiders may not be able to go outside, or if they do, they constantly worry about encountering a spider. They may experience a panic attack in the presence of a spider or even by seeing pictures of a spider! This fear is excessive and not proportional to the danger the person is actually facing. The brain is tricked into thinking there is significant, immediate danger where no danger exists.

Frequently, people will have more than one phobia at a time. In fact, 75 percent of people with a specific phobia will fear more than one situation or object, with an average of three phobias per person. For teens between the ages of 13 and 17, about 16 percent are affected by specific fears, and females experience phobias twice as often as males.

So, what causes these strange fears to develop? For most teens, the fear comes about for no specific reason, or at least not one they can remember. For some, though, a trauma that they personally experienced (for example, being stung by a swarm of wasps, or even just one) or that they saw someone else experience (for example, seeing someone being bitten by a dog) can be the reason a specific fear develops.

The good news is that most teenagers who develop phobias usually outgrow them by adulthood, and they can be free of the anxiety even sooner by breaking the cycle of avoidance and gradually facing these fears little by little. That's what you'll learn in this book! With the use of the coping skills we'll cover in the following sections, you will become more confident in managing anxiety that occurs with these specific fears.

Types of Phobias

As you can imagine, a person can have a phobia of almost anything! Phobias typically fall into two categories: those relating to situations and objects. Here are some examples of each:

Situations

* Decidophobia – Fear of making decisions

* Gelotophobia – Fear of being laughed at

* Haphephobia – Fear of being touched

* Nyctophobia – Fear of darkness

Objects

* Coulrophobia – Fear of clowns

* Cynophobia – Fear of dogs

* Dentophobia – Fear of dentists

* Dysmorphobia – Fearful obsession with a real or imaginary body flaw

Symptoms Checklist: Phobias

As we saw earlier, fears are common, and most people have a handful of things they are afraid of, but they aren't overly distressed by the fear. They go about their lives normally, and this fear doesn't cause them to avoid situations or places. If your fear is actually a phobia, you will likely . . .

☐ have intense fear of a specific situation or thing.

☐ experience anxiety/fear in this situation or thing (or even just thinking about it).

☐ try to avoid this specific object/situation, or if it cannot be avoided, endure it with intense fear.

☐ have a greater fear of the situation or object than what's necessary or expected.

☐ allow this fear to get in the way of your functioning at school, at home, in activities, or in some other important way.

Do any of these common symptoms apply to you? If so, what is the object or situation you fear most? Use the exercises in this book to tackle those phobias for good.

In Real Life

Chelsea's Vicious Cycle

When Chelsea was seven, she had a really bad case of the stomach flu. She got so sick that she was constantly vomiting and had to go to the hospital in an ambulance. She stayed in the hospital for a few days while doctors gave her fluids and food through a feeding tube. Being only seven years old, Chelsea was terrified by this whole experience.

Even now, at 13 years old, Chelsea still remembers how awful it was to throw up over and over again. She remembers thinking she was going to die. When the ambulance came, she remembers the wailing of sirens and all those people in uniforms touching her. Chelsea recovered fully from the flu, but to this day, anxiety overwhelms her when she thinks about throwing up. When she hears other people complain about feeling sick to their stomachs, she feels a surge of panic, fearing that she will catch what they have and that it will cause her to throw up, too. Chelsea often avoids hanging out with her friends outside of school for fear that she will get sick. Even when she hears an ambulance, she feels like she can't breathe and her heart races. She begs her mom to avoid driving by the hospital because she will panic if she sees or hears an ambulance. And when she can, she tries to get out of going to school.

When Chelsea eats too much, she gets confused about the feelings in her stomach and believes that she is coming down with an illness that will make her throw up—which of course makes her incredibly anxious. What's worse, this anxiety makes her actually feel nauseated! As a result, Chelsea eats too little, which leads to more nausea and abdominal pain and weakens her immune system, making her more likely to get sick. It's a vicious cycle!

Do you think Chelsea has a phobia? If so, what do you think her phobia is? Do you know what makes her issue a phobia rather than just an ordinary fear? Do you have any phobias similar to Chelsea's? What makes the feeling that you're experiencing more than "just a fear"?

Panic

The room starts spinning. Your heart beats louder and faster, pounding against your chest. You take big gasping breaths, yet you still feel like you can't breathe. You tremble and shake. You're sweating and shivering. The room is spinning as you feel yourself getting closer to passing out. You sit frozen, but your thoughts race and flood your mind. Your brain screams at you, "This is it! I'm dying! There is no way out! Everyone is watching as I pass out, or even die!" All the while, you sit there, powerless to end the torture.

This whirlwind of terrifying and physically uncomfortable feelings is called a panic attack, and it is surprisingly NORMAL. Your body is designed to do all the things I just described, not to hurt you, but to *protect* you. When something potentially dangerous occurs, your body is designed to go on alert. Have you ever heard of "fight or flight"? This response helps you react and keep yourself safe. For example, imagine you're in your backyard when you hear a scary hissing sound. You spot a snake slithering its way through the grass toward you. In this scenario, you would *want* your body to experience the symptoms of a panic attack. You would want your heart to beat fast to get the blood pumping to your arms and legs so you can get out of there as quickly as possible. You would want your breathing to increase to get as much oxygen to your brain and body as possible. And you would want your mind to race, so it could quickly decide the best course of action. It's called the fight-or-flight response because your body is now prepared to either react to the danger (fight) or get you quickly to safety (flight).

Sometimes, though, our bodies trigger this fight-or-flight response just from thinking about something we fear, or it happens completely out of the blue when no real danger is present. When this happens, your brain tries to understand why your body is freaking out. And your brain usually reacts with some far-fetched conclusion like "The world is ending!" or "I'm definitely dying!"

According to the research, teens are more likely to experience panic attacks than other age groups. No surprise there! You face unique pressures and emotional changes that happen throughout your teen years. Academic demands and expectations are high. Relationships can be complex, confusing, and overwhelming. You're trying to gain some independence from your parents and want more freedom. The list goes on. All this uncertainty can lead to worries and fears that trigger panic attacks, even if you don't realize what's causing them.

Here's the good news: Panic attacks cannot kill you, even if you feel like they might! No one has ever died from a panic attack, and you will certainly not be the first. If you can keep your mind in check and your breathing steady, you can control a panic attack, making it shorter and less intense. In part 2 of the book you'll do some exercises that will help you learn this skill.

Types of Panic

Panic can be experienced once in your life, never to be felt again, or it can happen many times. Panic sensations can come out of nowhere or be triggered by something distressing. The type of panic you may be experiencing depends on two things: the intensity of the fear, and how frequently it happens. The two main types of panic are these:

* Panic Attack

* Panic Disorder

PANIC ATTACK

Panic attacks are sudden bursts of fear, sometimes accompanied by physical discomfort. This discomfort typically peaks within 10 minutes (often less) and then slowly wears off. Teen panic attacks are often triggered by stressful situations such as an exam or presentation, a new social situation, or a negative interaction with friends, parents, or teachers.

When a trigger (say a big test) causes the panic attack, it can be easy to understand what's happening to you (*This test is super important, so I'm really starting to stress*) and therefore easier to control (*I studied. It's an open-book test. Take a deep breath.*).

However, panic sensations can sometimes come from out of the blue with no apparent reason at all. You might experience waves of fear, a racing heart, and rapid breathing that can lead you to believe you are dying, going crazy, or about to pass out. In reality, you are perfectly safe, but your body and mind are being tricked, and the sensations are so intense that it is hard to believe that you are safe while these things are happening to you. We'll explore strategies for how to control panic and reduce the intensity of these feelings.

PANIC DISORDER

Just like a panic attack, panic disorder is the experience of sudden sensations of fear and sometimes physical discomfort. However, many teens begin to develop a powerful fear of having more panic attacks—this fear is the very reason panic attacks persist! They may worry so much about having another panic attack that they avoid doing things they would usually do. For example, if you had a panic attack in algebra class during an exam, you may fear having more panic attacks in that class and begin skipping class. Your fear may be so intense that you attempt to avoid school altogether. You may convince yourself that you will pass out or die if you have another panic attack. You may worry that your classmates will make fun of you or think you are crazy. You believe that if you avoid the situation, that will solve the problem. The problem with avoidance is that it prevents you from having a positive experience to counteract the fear. For example, if you had a panic attack at a school dance, it would be important to follow up with a positive social experience, like a good time at another dance or a party, so you could be reassured that you're able to stay cool in social situations. It's important to follow a panic attack with positive experiences to teach your brain that you're safe and in control. Learning what panic sensations are and knowing that they can't harm you is an important part of stopping the cycle of fear.

Symptoms Checklist: Panic

Panic attacks look different for each person, but most people who have panic attacks experience four or more of the common sensations listed here. What does a panic attack look like for you? Check the box next to the sensations you have experienced:

☐ Rapid or pounding heart

☐ Shortness of breath

☐ Feeling flush, hot in the face, sweating

☐ Chills or cold sweats

☐ Trembling or shaking

☐ Feelings of choking

☐ Chest pain or weight pushing on your chest

☐ Nausea or discomfort in your stomach

☐ Dizziness or faintness

☐ Numbness or tingling in your arms or legs

☐ Feeling disconnected from your surroundings or yourself

☐ Fear that you are losing control or "going crazy"

☐ Fear of dying

If you know what a panic attack looks like for you, these signs can help you identify when a panic attack is happening or about to happen. Knowing that gives you the power to start calming yourself earlier to gain control over your symptoms.

Kyle Is Driven by Panic

Kyle is 16 and just got his driver's license. He's excited that he is the first of his friends to begin driving, and he got a new truck and can't wait to show it off. He takes his truck out for the first time without his parents or a driving instructor. As he cruises around his neighborhood, he suddenly starts to feel hot and sweaty. His heart starts beating wildly. He is trembling and feels like he can't breathe. He swerves and almost hits a mailbox. He feels like he can't focus and is about to pass out. He manages to bring the truck to a stop, but he starts to think that he is having a heart attack and may die. The feelings he's going through are torturous, but after about 10 minutes they start to subside, and gradually he returns to normal, though he is completely shaken. Kyle has never experienced anything like this before. He has no idea what to think. Why did this happen? He was excited about driving, so why, out of nowhere, did he all of a sudden feel so anxious? Was he really having a heart attack? And should he go to the hospital?

As a result of this situation, Kyle is afraid to drive again. He carefully drives home and tells his parents he needs to see a doctor. He worries that if he drives again, he will have another, similar, experience. When his mom makes him drive to school a few days later, Kyle again starts breathing rapidly and can feel his heart pounding the whole way to school. What was once the most exciting thing in his life, he now faces with dread.

Kyle's experience is unfortunately really common and shows how panic attacks can come from out of the blue and ruin what would otherwise be fun experiences. While Kyle was initially focused on the excitement of driving, some part of his mind and body were focused on the newness and pressure of driving. Without Kyle's knowledge, that part of his mind sent out a danger signal, and his body responded by trying to get Kyle out of danger—to stop driving the car! The problem, though, is that Kyle wasn't actually in danger, so his body's response felt strange and was confusing to him. Kyle misinterpreted what was happening to his body as a possible heart attack or death. This impression made the panic attack last longer, and it has left him too scared to drive again.

Going forward, how can Kyle think about this situation more realistically? How can Kyle act or think differently to feel less anxious?

Myths and Truths: The Straight Scoop on Anxiety

People often have misconceptions about anxiety and what it means to experience it, especially since anxiety can look so different from person to person. Here are some common myths about anxiety, followed by the truth:

Myth: Anxiety is not common; I am alone.
Truth: More of your peers than you know are struggling with anxiety, though it may look different for each person. The reason it feels like you are alone is that many people keep their anxiety hidden and don't talk about it.

Nearly one out of three of your peers has struggled with significant anxiety at some point! Adolescence is a tough time with many changes and new experiences, so it's not surprising that significant anxiety is an emotion often described by teens.

Myth: Anxiety is bad and should be eliminated.
Truth: Anxiety can be helpful!

There is such a thing as "just the right amount" of anxiety. Your body was designed to feel anxiety to keep you safe. In today's world, safety comes in more forms than just hunting for food and fighting off bear attacks. Today, safety can mean performing well at school, having safe and happy relationships, and taking care of your physical body. When a small amount of anxiety pushes you to take care of yourself, your relationships, your mind, and your body, then you know you have just enough!

For example, you might worry about how to break some bad news to your best friend. That means that you care about your friend's feelings and are working toward taking care of your friendship. Being so worried about breaking bad news to a friend that you stop talking to them and avoid interacting with them means you have too much anxiety! Anxiety should help you manage difficult situations and protect what's important to you. Avoidance is often a signal that the anxiety is more than it should be.

Myth: Anxiety will ruin my life; I won't be successful.
Truth: Anxiety can actually fuel success when it is harnessed and channeled appropriately.

As described in the last truth, some anxiety can help you work harder, concentrate better, and dedicate yourself to the things you care about. The trick is to be in control of your anxiety rather than letting it overwhelm and control you. By using the tools you'll learn in part 2 of this book, you'll have the ability to manage and control anxiety, and even channel it to help you reach your goals.

Myth: If I am perfect, I will feel less anxious.

Truth: Mistakes are okay! Trying to be perfect and avoid mistakes will definitely not reduce your anxiety. Studying for hours and hours after school, pulling all-nighters, and trying to get a perfect score will not make the worry and stress about school go away. In fact, doing that can have the opposite effect. Later in the book we'll talk about perfectionism and why it can make anxiety worse. You'll learn how to focus on your efforts and embrace mistakes—an important part of harnessing anxiety to help you feel more confident and calm.

How NOT to Cope

For some people, anxiety can come from out of nowhere and be intense and overwhelming. But for others, it's a feeling that lingers and is present almost all day, every day. Either way, when anxiety gets to be too much, it can be physically painful and mentally exhausting and leave you desperate for immediate relief. When you don't know how to make it go away, it's easy to resort to unhealthy or unhelpful coping tools to try and feel better. Some common not-so-helpful strategies for reducing anxiety include the following:

Avoidance

As we discussed, avoiding the situation often makes anxiety worse in the long run. It prevents you from being able to have positive and healthy experiences that communicate to your brain that your anxious thoughts are not realistic or necessary. Avoidance can trap you in an anxious cycle that is hard to break.

Perfectionism

You may think you will feel less anxious if you achieve perfection: a 100 on your test, the team captain, student council president, the top 10 percent of the class, and so on. By achieving perfection, you will avoid the catastrophe your mind believes will happen—failure. But, rationally speaking, perfection is impossible to achieve. By expecting yourself to be perfect, you will undoubtedly feel more anxious when you are a normal human and make mistakes, like we all do.

Rumination

Rumination is when you think about something over and over and over again. You might believe that if you think about something enough, you will find an answer or way out of your fears. You may allow your mind to obsess over your fears and potential disasters as a way to figure out a solution. The problem with this strategy is that many fears are irrational or unlikely to become reality. Focusing on fear only communicates to your brain that there is something to worry about. This strengthens the connection in your brain between the anxiety and the trigger.

Compulsions

Compulsions are when you feel like you need to do something, in this case to make the anxious distress go away. For example, checking that your door is locked several times in order to feel safe in your home—that's compulsive. You may feel the need to do this before you can relax, and it means you're not trusting your own brain. Plus, compulsions are a temporary fix. Even though you feel like you're taking action against your fear, this behavior ultimately communicates to your brain that you have something to fear and that the danger is real. Therefore, the anxiety will return over and over again unless you break the cycle.

Controlling

Many anxious teens can be described as controlling or inflexible. You may have trouble going with the flow or dealing with it when things don't go as planned. Perhaps you fear that the worst will happen and by controlling everything around you, you might prevent disaster. What's wrong with this? Well, inevitably things don't go as planned, the world throws us curveballs, people are unpredictable, and you just can't control everything. Of course, when the unpredictable happens, you become even more anxious because you weren't able to foresee it. The brain is now more convinced than ever that the worst will happen, and your anxiety continues.

Self-Medicating with Substances

It is tempting for some people to try and dull the physical and mental discomfort of anxiety. Turning to substances like alcohol or drugs is unfortunately common, and it is incredibly unhelpful. It prevents you from having the opportunity to work through the anxiety and feel successful in doing so. Learning to work through problems as a teen is an important thing—this sets the foundation for problem-solving skills you'll need throughout your life. Substance use is a temporary fix that never lasts and has a long list of risks and negative consequences. If you find that you are regularly using substances to dull your distress, please do the brave thing by reaching out to a trusted person in your life and asking for support.

So now you know some of the ways not to cope. Be sure to read on, as the following sections will arm you with more helpful and healthy tools for battling anxiety, so you can let go of any unhelpful coping behaviors once and for all!

Facing Anxiety

You may groan at this, but gradually facing anxiety is really important. Facing anxiety increases your ability to deal with distress and increases your confidence when facing challenges. In short, it makes you stronger. But there's no need to jump into the deep end of the pool without first learning how to swim. We'll start small, and then gradually do more and more. It takes time, repetition, and patience to learn anything new—yep, practice makes perfect. You may find that the strategies in the following sections offer some immediate relief, but to really conquer anxiety in the long run, your brain has to learn to use these tools by repeating them over and over again, even if they seem to not work right away.

As you read on and start to put these strategies into practice, try to think of creative ways you can challenge yourself to face your fears, a little at a time.

How to Get Help

Call for Backup!

This book is designed to help you gain control over anxious thoughts, feelings, and behaviors. But sometimes anxiety is too much to deal with on your own, no matter how hard you try! How do you know if you need to seek extra support? Check the statements that apply to you. If you check any of the boxes, try talking to your parents, teachers, or a school counselor about getting some backup:

I can't concentrate at school and my grades are significantly impacted.

I avoid school and try to stay home as often as possible, and/or my school is concerned about my attendance.

I have panic attacks almost every day and don't want to leave the house.

I am losing my friends, or my relationships are really suffering because of my anxiety.

I feel like I need to use alcohol or drugs to stop these feelings.

I just can't take the stress and worry any longer and need a way out.

I have thoughts about harming myself to make the stress go away.

Reading this book is a great step in the right direction. But remember, no one can be perfect, and even the most successful people have a team of people who support them. The president has a staff, surgeons have nurses and fellow doctors, quarterbacks have linemen and receivers, teachers have aides, and music artists have entourages of people helping them. Everyone can benefit if they use the supports around them. Getting support to overcome anxiety is no different. Be brave enough to call in your team for backup!

If you are having thoughts about harming yourself or suicide, take action immediately! Your mind is trying to tell you it needs more help, so please call in reinforcements. Talk to someone right away, call 9-1-1, or get to your closest emergency room to get people who can really help. Professionals are trained to help and want to support you.

Who are the people you would put on *your* team? Think about parents, aunts and uncles, close friends, teachers, mentors, religious leaders, coaches, tutors, school counselors, psychologists, psychiatrists, pediatricians, and family friends. List at least three people who you believe could encourage you as you work through this challenge.

You *Can* Feel Better

In parts 2 and 3 of the book, you'll learn tools that have the power to influence emotions. As you know, emotions can be really difficult to control. They are not like a light switch that you can turn on and off as you please—how easy would that be? Once negative emotions take over, it's easy to feel like they are completely controlling you and you are powerless. However, years of research and practice have shown us two areas that are really effective in influencing emotions: our thoughts and our actions. Think of a triangle with emotions, thoughts, and actions at each point. When you make a change to one, it's been proven to affect the other two.

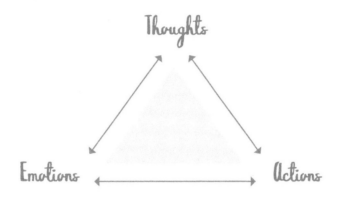

You can now see that certain ways of thinking (assuming the worst will happen, misinterpreting your body's sensations, not believing in your abilities) and behaving (avoiding situations) can trigger anxiety or keep anxiety going. It makes sense, then, that thinking and behaving differently could reduce anxiety—and it does! As you read on, you will learn strategies and activities that will help you think and act in ways that ease anxious feelings. As you practice these strategies and activities, you'll gain the power to override your emotions and even use anxiety to your advantage!

" Be quiet! "

Part Two

CALMING YOUR ANXIOUS MIND

"Just don't worry about it! Get over it and move on!" Can you relate to this unhelpful advice? Some of your well-meaning friends and family may have given you such advice in response to your anxiety. Clearly, they don't really understand what it's like to have an anxious mind! If stopping anxious thoughts were so easy, this book would not exist.

Part 2 will teach you truly helpful strategies for calming your mind, tackling unhelpful thinking patterns, and reshaping your thoughts to be more realistic and confident. In short, these tools can help you feel so much better, especially the more you practice them.

Exercise 1: It's a Zoo!

The feelings of anxiety can make you feel like you're living in a zoo, or even a jungle. Think about it! Are the thoughts in your mind chaotic, loud, and sometimes scary? Perhaps you can envision a brain full of beasts roaring at you and causing fear? Anxiety can often feel that overwhelming, flooding you with fearful thoughts that just seem to get louder and louder. It can be hard to contain the noise and dismiss the fear when all you really want is a peaceful space in your mind.

The first step to ridding your brain of these loud and demanding thoughts is to identify them. What are the thoughts that are occupying your mental space? On the following lines, take a moment to jot down the anxious thoughts that you typically have. No need to filter anything out—say it all, and try to get down anything that causes any amount of anxiety. Think of it as a "brain dump," unloading your brain of all the anxious garbage as you transfer it to paper.

_____

_____

_____

_____

_____

_____

_____

_____

_____

_____

_____

Now that you have completed your brain dump, look through the list. Rate each item. On a scale of 0 to 100 percent, how much anxiety does each one cause you? What's at the top of your anxiety sources? Do you notice a pattern or theme in your worries? Are they all about school? Are they more about social situations? Or do they vary, with worries about all sorts of things?

As you begin to work through your anxious thinking in the rest of this section, try picking some of the worries that are rated in the middle of your list. You can begin to practice tools you can use with these anxious thoughts. They might become easier to tackle as you get used to using the tools. As you become more confident with the different strategies, you can start to tackle the worries at the top of your list.

Exercise 2: **Brain Spam**

How long can you go without thinking any thoughts? Not long, right? It's okay—the brain processes thoughts constantly. Some thoughts are useful and important ("Don't forget to study for the Spanish quiz."), some thoughts are fun ("Can't wait to binge-watch my show tonight!"), some thoughts are weird or silly ("I wonder what it would be like to be best friends with a celebrity."), and some thoughts are scary ("What if there is a zombie apocalypse?"). Part of the brain's job is to sort through all these thoughts and determine which ones are important enough to focus on and do something about, and which thoughts are like spam in your e-mail, or unwanted ads in your social media feed. Spam thoughts are distracting but often not important, not worth paying much attention to, or so outlandish that they should really be blocked out completely. Of the examples above, the thought about an impending zombie apocalypse is probably the most obvious spam thought—incredibly unlikely to happen and not worth your energy or worry.

But sometimes the brain gets confused or stuck and doesn't do the best job of sorting through and filtering out the spam thoughts. The brain chooses to focus on the zombie apocalypse. It is tricked into thinking the zombies are probably coming after you soon, and the anxiety of how to survive in a postapocalyptic world takes over. The brain just glitches and can no longer tell if this is something you really need to worry about or if these thoughts are ridiculous and need to be trashed.

Take a moment to write down some thoughts that your brain may have kept in your mental inbox that should have been marked as spam. What are the dumb ads and junk mail that take up space in your mind? Which thoughts are actually important to you or worth some amount of worry or anxiety? Go ahead and divide these thoughts between the inbox and the spam folder.

SPAM

_____

_____

_____

_____

_____

_____

_____

INBOX

_____

_____

_____

_____

_____

_____

_____

Exercise 3: Taking Charge of Your Anxious Alter Ego

Sometimes anxious thoughts can seem like the very loud and demanding voice of an anxious alter ego, or that of a supervillain seeking doom and destruction! It's as if the thoughts are not your own and the distress and anxiety caused by this voice is overwhelming. It's so pushy that you can't hear your own realistic, calm thoughts.

Funny as it may sound, one strategy that can begin to give you power over this anxious and negative voice is to give it a name and start to talk back to it. No, seriously. Rather than believe the anxious alter ego, you will begin to challenge it and tell yourself (and it) that it is not your true voice.

Brainstorm an identity to give to your anxious alter ego. Try drawing it in the space provided here, and give it a name. Whatever—Nervous Nelly, Bully Bob, or maybe just go with something silly like Sir Arnold Speakstoomuch. Be creative!

Name of Your Anxious Alter Ego Here:

_____

How does your anxious alter ego bully you or try to take charge? What kinds of thoughts do you associate with your anxious alter ego?

_____

_____

_____

How does your anxious alter ego make your life more difficult? How does it prevent you from having fun or being confident?

_____

_____

_____

What are some things you could say to challenge and fight the alter ego into submission? Go ahead and be mean—don't hold back!

_____

_____

_____

As you work toward combating the anxious voice and thoughts, the goal is to gradually shrink the alter ego, making the alter ego voice quieter and quieter, and your own confident and calm voice louder and louder.

Certain thoughts and actions can make the anxious alter ego louder—think of it like food and energy you give to the alter ego that keep it strong. Things that feed the alter ego are the unhelpful coping strategies discussed in part 1: avoidance, perfectionism, rumination, compulsions, controlling, and self-medicating. Engaging in these patterns keeps the anxious voice strong and powerful. This is why it's important to practice these strategies—to shrink and destroy your anxious alter ego.

Exercise 4: **Thinking Errors**

Another trick that the anxious alter ego uses is that it manipulates the way you think. There are certain ways of thinking that can trick the mind into believing something that isn't completely true. This thinking tends to lead to unnecessary anxiety. We call these unhelpful thinking patterns "thinking errors." Following is a list of some common thinking errors with a description of each. Place a check by the thinking errors you can relate to, and see if you can come up with an example of how you used one recently:

☐ **All-or-Nothing Thinking**

Seeing things only as black and white, being unable to see other explanations or scenarios

An example: "If I don't get a 100 on this test, I am a failure." (even though an 89 is not failing!)

Your example:

_____

_____

_____

☐ **Overgeneralizing**

Using one bad experience to describe all experiences

An example: "I *never* score a goal in soccer!" (even though it's only your second game OR you have made goals many times in the past)

Your example:

_____

_____

_____

☐ **Mental Filtering**

Paying attention to only one bit of input that confirms what you already believe about yourself while filtering out all information that may say otherwise

An example: Sally said she likes your outfit today. Sarah asked you where you got your awesome shoes. But Jared gave you a weird look today. You remember only Jared's weird look and filter out all the positive feedback you received. This makes you feel sad, anxious, and self-conscious.

Your example:

_____

_____

_____

☐ **Jumping to Conclusions**

Believing you know what others are thinking or that you can predict what will happen in the future

An example: When you walked into class, two popular students looked in your direction. You assume they are thinking how weird or ugly you look. But, in reality, you don't know what they are thinking at all!

Your example:

_____

_____

_____

☐ **Magnification/Catastrophizing**

Blowing things out of proportion

An example: "If I don't get a 1400 on my SATs, I won't get into college, I won't get a job, everyone will think I'm stupid, I will never make any money, and I will live forever alone and homeless!"

Your example:

_____

_____

_____

☐ **Emotional Reasoning**

Assuming your feelings are accurate and that there is evidence for those feelings

An example: "I feel embarrassed—everyone must think I'm the weirdest person!"

Continued . . .

Exercise 4 Cont.: **Thinking Errors**

Your example:

_____

_____

_____

☐ **Should/Must Statements**

Using words like "I should do this" or "I must achieve this" that make you feel guilty and like a failure

An example: "I should have done better at choir tryouts. I should have practiced more! I should have known I would suck!"

Your example:

_____

_____

_____

☐ **Labeling**

Calling yourself names or labeling yourself (or others) negatively

An example: "I'm such a loser."

Your example:

_____

_____

_____

☐ **Personalizing**

Blaming yourself for things that may not be entirely your responsibility

An example: Taking the complete blame for a group project not being finished in time, even though other group members were partly responsible for the outcome

Your example:

_____

_____

_____

QUIZ: *Thinking Errors*

See if you can use your memory of the last exercise to identify which thinking error is being used. And definitely no need to get anxious—this is just a fun little self-test to see how much you remember. Why? Well, knowing these thinking errors well will help you catch yourself using them in the act! This can help you put a stop to anxious thinking right in the moment.

Kathryn got her algebra test grade back—an 87. Kathryn is used to getting As. She starts to panic as she thinks about her GPA dropping, then about not getting into college, then about not getting her dream job, then about being poor and living alone with just her cats to comfort her!

What thinking error(s) do you think Kathryn is using?

_____

_____

_____

Kyndal plays the clarinet in the school marching band. She missed a note, and her clarinet made an awful squeak! She felt embarrassed and stupid for making such a loud mistake. Kyndal knows that everyone heard it and they are thinking she doesn't deserve to be in the band. She can tell that the band director doesn't think she has any talent and is going to hold this against her.

What thinking error(s) do you think Kyndal is using?

_____

_____

_____

Continued . . .

Quiz Cont.: *Thinking Errors*

Patrick went to a youth group that a lot of his peers from school attend. It was his first time, and he was nervous. He met up with several people who he knows are pretty cool. He told a few jokes, and everyone laughed, except for one guy. At the end of the night, everyone was friendly and said goodbye and told him they would see him tomorrow at school. But when Patrick got home, he could not stop thinking about the one guy who dissed him. It made him feel embarrassed and self-conscious. Now he doesn't want to go back to the youth group because he feels like he didn't make a good impression.

What thinking error(s) do you think Patrick is using?

_____

_____

_____

_____

Exercise 5: **Thoughts on Trial**

You know that anxious thoughts trick your mind into believing things that are unlikely or unrealistic. Your anxious alter ego uses thinking errors to keep you stuck in emotional quicksand. So how do you know which thoughts you should believe and which you should filter out as brain spam? One way to see if your thoughts are worth worrying about or if they are an alter ego trick is to put your thoughts on trial.

During a trial, lawyers present evidence for and against a claim to determine the most likely reality. A judge or jury then decides if the claim is believable or not. You can also use this technique with your anxious thoughts.

Here's an example:

Anxious Thought: I'm going to die in a plane crash when I go to Hawaii this summer.	
EVIDENCE FOR (THOUGHT IS REALISTIC)	**EVIDENCE AGAINST (THOUGHT IS NOT REALISTIC)**
I've seen news coverage about plane crashes. My uncle was on a plane one time that had to make an emergency landing. There are tons of movies about plane crashes, so it must be something many people worry about. Flying to Hawaii takes like eight hours; that's a long time for something to potentially go wrong.	The news covers plane crashes only because they are so rare that's it's kind of crazy when it happens! My uncle's pilot made safe choices, and everyone on his plane was fine. Movies are fiction and dramatized—not real life. There are hundreds of flights a day, every day, for years and years, that make it to Hawaii with no problem! Therefore, the chances of something going wrong are very slim. Pilots are trained professionals, and the flight crews know how to keep us safe. Even if there were problems with the plane, there are tons of backup safety procedures and mechanisms that keep the plane perfectly safe. A quick Internet search shows that the odds of a plane crash are 1 in 11 million! That's a .000009% chance. This makes flying the SAFEST mode of transportation!
Verdict: Anxious thought not realistic	

Continued . . .

Exercise 5 Cont.: **Thoughts on Trial**

> **More Realistic Thought:** I am very safe when flying, and the chances of anything going wrong are so slim that it's not worth the worry! So I'm gonna sit back, relax, and enjoy eight hours of Netflix and video games.

    Try practicing with a thought of your own. What is the evidence for and against it, and what is the most likely verdict based on the evidence? Once you have all the evidence, write a thought that is more realistic.

Anxious Thought:	
EVIDENCE FOR (THOUGHT IS REALISTIC)	**EVIDENCE AGAINST** (THOUGHT IS NOT REALISTIC)
Verdict:	
More Realistic Thought:	

Exercise 6: **Worst-Case Scenario**

Your anxious alter ego likely encourages you to fantasize about the worst possible outcomes. Your mind will take you to the deepest depths of destruction and despair—it is just ridiculous! The good news is that your mind is very creative. That's a skill you can harness and channel into healthier pursuits! The bad news is that if you believe these anxious and terrifying thoughts are real and definitely going to happen, it can be a terrible burden. So if your mind is going to think about the worst-case scenario, you might as well go ahead and answer the question "What's the worst that could happen?"

Let's try it! Pick one of your anxious thoughts from Exercise 1 (page 26). Write the thought in the following space and then write the worst-case scenario. What's the absolute worst that could happen? Here's an example to help:

An example: The homecoming dance

> **Anxious thought:** I won't have a date for homecoming.
> **Worst-case scenario:** *I'll have to stay at home by myself, miss all the fun, and everyone will think I'm a loser.*

Your example:

> **Anxious thought:**

_____

_____

_____

_____

> **Worst-case scenario:**

_____

_____

_____

_____

Continued . . .

Exercise 6 Cont.: **Worst-Case Scenario**

Okay, now you have identified the worst possible thing that could happen (even if it is very unlikely). Next, answer a few questions:

1. If the worst thing happened, so what? Would it be so bad?

An example: I mean, yeah, it would stink to not enjoy the dance with a date, but I guess it wouldn't be THAT bad.

Your example:

_____

_____

_____

_____

2. If the worst thing happened, is there anything I could do about it? Are there any solutions?

An example: I could go to the dance anyway and try to have fun with friends who don't have dates. Or I could invite the other solos over to my house, watch bad movies, and make fun of how lame the dance probably is. Or I could just get into some comfy pj's, eat ice cream, and be thankful that I don't have to wear uncomfortable dress clothes!

Your example:

_____

_____

_____

_____

3. If the worst thing happened, how would I handle it?

An example: I can't do anything about what others think of me, but surely I'm not the only person who doesn't have a date to homecoming. I can do my best to have fun or treat myself in some other way. It's not very likely that anyone is thinking bad things about me; people are probably far too focused on themselves.

Your example:

_____

_____

_____

_____

4. If the worst thing happened, will I still be okay?

An example: Yeah, I think I'll get over it. Homecoming buzz will pass in a few days, and no one will be thinking about it anymore.

Your example:

_____

_____

_____

_____

Often, the anxious alter ego tricks us into believing the worst-case scenario is both horrible and certain to occur, and leaves us feeling helpless. But, in reality, if we answer the question "If the worst happens, what will I do about it?" we see that there are almost always remedies for these problems. So you actually do have the ability and power to do something to help yourself. Shift all that creativity to thinking of solutions for these supposed worst-case scenarios. Once you've done that, the anxiety usually lifts and feels much less powerful, because now you're focused on solutions rather than the problem. You're in control now, so pat yourself on the back—your alter ego has just lost some of its power!

Exercise 1: Do the Math

You're sitting in math class, and your mind drifts to the thought "When will I ever need to know this stuff?!" Well, here it is! Time to put that math to good use. Anxious thoughts can often be quashed with a little bit of statistics and probability. When an anxious thought appears or a worst-case scenario is taking control, stop and do a little math. Ask yourself, "What's the likelihood of this happening?" or "What are the chances?" Once you assign a real number to it, you'll realize you are far safer than your anxious alter ego wants you to realize.

Here's an example:

You're in bed at night, trying to put your mind at ease and get some sleep. You hear a thump. *What is that? Someone's breaking in! They are going to hurt us! OMG, this is the end!!!*

Okay, so let's do the statistics. What are the chances that the bump you heard is a thief in the night? What are the chances that the bump is your dad getting a late-night snack? Or your little sister getting out of bed to play with her toys while your parents sleep? Consider the odds:

* Thieves have broken into my house 0 times in the 15 years I have lived here:

    365 nights per year × 15 years = 5,475 nights

    0 break-ins out of 5,475 nights (0/5,475) = 0%

* Thieves have broken into my neighbors' houses 0 times in the 15 years I have lived here: 0/5,475 = 0%

* I have heard Mom or Dad up and about in the house at night at least 100 times in the 15 years I have lived here: 100/5,475 = 1.8%

* I have heard my siblings up and about in the house at night at least 100 times in the 15 years I have lived here: 100/5,475 = 1.8%

* I have heard other things make noise in this house, like the A/C unit coming on, the dishwasher starting up, the dryer banging around with clothes, the refrigerator making ice cubes, and the dog or cat creeping around. These things have happened all the time in the past 15 years I have lived here—okay, let's not even try to do that math! Safe to assume IT'S MUCH MORE LIKELY!

Try this for yourself. Pick an anxious thought from Exercise 1 (page 26) and run some statistics.

Anxious thought:

_____

_____

_____

_____

Likelihood/percentage/probability it will happen:

_____

_____

_____

_____

Other explanations and the likelihoods/percentages they will happen:

_____

_____

_____

_____

Quiz: *Why Are Thoughts Important?*

Scenario: You're at school, and you see your friend Megan as you pass her in the hallway. You say, "Hey!" and Megan keeps walking and doesn't say anything back. Circle the letter below that matches the first thought that came to your mind as to why Megan ignored you:

a. She is mad at me. I must have done something to upset her, and now she hates me!

b. She must not have heard me. It's super crowded and loud in these halls!

c. She must have something on her mind that has her really distracted.

If you chose "a," you came to the same conclusion that many other anxious teens immediately come to. Let's go one step further. For each of these thoughts, list the emotion you feel:

a. _____

b. _____

c. _____

As you can see, each thought is a possible explanation for Megan's behavior. But each thought triggers a very different emotion. You probably associated option "a" with something like anxiety or sadness. But is option "a" the most likely reason your friend didn't say *hi* to you? Do you have enough information to reach that conclusion? Are there things you can do to find out before you decide to be anxious or sad?

Thoughts are important because they can powerfully influence our feelings, especially feelings of anxiety. Do the next few exercises in this section and see which ones are best at helping you reframe your thoughts in a more positive way.

Exercise 8: **Gray Thoughts**

As you see from the quiz we just did, how you look at a situation predicts the emotions you will probably experience. When your anxious alter ego is in control, you are likely to jump to conclusions that make you upset. It's important to ask yourself, "What other possible explanations are there?" Most situations have several explanations or outcomes, and it helps to consider these, too, instead of just assuming the worst outcome is the only possibility. You can also regard this as thinking in the "gray area" rather than only in black and white. The truth rarely lies in the extreme explanations; usually, the most realistic and likely explanations are somewhere in the middle. Get creative and see if you can find other possible explanations for situations that have caused you anxiety.

Here's an example:

Charlie tries out for the lead role in the fall theatrical production. There are only a handful of roles to give out this year, so Charlie is feeling pretty anxious. Charlie's director often praises him, but he is a strict and passionate director, which sometimes intimidates Charlie. Charlie completes his audition and feels pretty good about it. He's thinking he may get the lead role, even though he is only a sophomore and there are other senior actors who tried out and gave solid audition performances. When the results are posted, Charlie sees that he did not get the lead role. In fact, Charlie did not get any role! He is devastated. His initial thoughts are: "Wow, I'm a terrible actor." "The director must really hate me." "I can't audition again—this is humiliating!" "Maybe I should drop out of theater."

What other explanations could there be to account for Charlie's not being chosen for a role?

Here are some "gray thoughts" to consider:

* Lead roles probably went to the senior actors, as they have more experience, and this is their last chance at a play—it has nothing to do with Charlie's audition performance.

* Charlie just wasn't right for this particular role because he wasn't the type of character that was needed. When a more suitable role comes along, Charlie is sure to be cast.

* There were so many great actors auditioning, but only a few roles to hand out. Charlie did great, but not every great actor could get a role.

* Everyone, including the director, thought Charlie's performance was great, but other things outside of Charlie's control led to the director's decision.

Continued . . .

Exercise 8 Cont.: **Gray Thoughts**

If Charlie were to consider some of these gray thoughts, he would likely change his emotion from embarrassed, anxious, and sad to something more like calm, content, accepting, and encouraged to try again.

Think about a situation where you felt anxious. What were your initial conclusions? What other explanations or gray thoughts could you have considered? How do these thoughts change the way you feel?

Anxious situation:

_____

_____

_____

Anxious thoughts:

_____

_____

_____

Emotions:

_____

_____

_____

Gray thoughts:

_____

_____

_____

New emotions:

_____

_____

_____

Exercise 9: **Keeping It Real**

By now you know that anxious thinking is typically unhelpful and uncomfortable. But how many times have you heard the advice "Think positive!" Ugh, eye roll! That can be annoying advice because not everything that happens is positive. Some situations are just too difficult to find something positive about them. And it's hard to always see the bright side of a situation. The world is not a constant parade of rainbows and butterflies, right?

But wait. The goal of beating anxious thoughts is NOT to always be thinking positively—it's to be thinking REALISTICALLY. For example, if you have five final exams this week and two of them are on the same day, of course it would be easy to have some anxious thoughts and kind of hard to find the positive in all that. Your anxious thoughts might be: "I can't do this." "This is totally unfair—I don't have enough time." "I'm going to fail." "If I fail these tests, I won't pass the classes and I will have to repeat the grade!" If you were to force yourself to say positive thoughts, it would probably sound pretty ridiculous: "I'm going to make a 100 on all five of these tests!" "I'm so smart, I could do this in my sleep—I don't even need to study!" These thoughts are probably just as unrealistic and unlikely as the anxious thoughts.

Take a moment to jot down some realistic thoughts about this situation:

_____

_____

_____

_____

_____

_____

_____

_____

_____

Some realistic thoughts you might have written down are: "I plan to study as hard as I can with the time I have." "I've never failed a test before, so I am unlikely to fail now." "It's going to be a tough week, but I'll study as hard as I can and talk to my teachers if I am concerned." "If for some reason I fail one or more of these tests, there are probably things I can work out with my teachers to bring my grade up."

Continued . . .

Exercise 9 Cont.: Keeping It Real

Think of a time when you could have thought about a situation more realistically. Try to write down unrealistic thoughts you may have had, both anxious and positive. Then try to reframe your thoughts to be more realistic.

Situation:

_____

_____

_____

Anxious thoughts:

_____

_____

_____

Positive thoughts:

_____

_____

_____

Realistic thoughts:

_____

_____

_____

Now, of course, if you can find some real positivity in a situation, that's the best option, so go for it! But when times are tough, trying to find some realistic thoughts is sure to at least free you up from the distress of anxious thinking.

Exercise 10: **Fake News**

One important thing to know about worries is that they lie! Our anxious thoughts are usually deceitful and full of dramatization, like fake news! As we discussed earlier, your anxious thoughts are distorted by thinking errors and your own creativity. The more creative you are, the more you are able to create some amazing works of fiction in your mind. Like, could you imagine that when you try to talk to your crush, they look at you like you're an idiot and then point and laugh, yelling at the whole school to laugh at you for daring to talk to them! Yikes! Yes, that would be brutally mortifying. But is it real? Is it likely to really go down that way? Or is your anxious alter ego dramatizing the situation and keeping you too scared to get a date? So it's important to know that worries lie to you, and they take advantage of your own creativity to do it.

Here are a few ways to combat fake news:

Let thoughts just be thoughts. Obviously, every thought that enters your mind is NOT true. Practice telling yourself, "This is just a thought. It's creative and would make a great movie, but it's not real."

Use your creativity differently. You clearly have an intelligent and creative mind. Use these skills to bring out a different emotion, like joy! Imagine alternative ways the situation could play out. Turn your horror film into a comedy or a romance.

Let the thought pass. Since every thought isn't worth your time and attention, start practicing letting some of the thoughts pass through you. Think of it like channel surfing—some channels and shows are not worth stopping for. You notice that it's there and see that it's not worth your time, so you keep clicking on through. Imagine hitting the channel changer on your mental remote control when an unhelpful anxious thought comes to you. Next, next. Keep clicking through until you land on a thought that brings out a more relaxing or positive emotion.

Exercise 11: Worry Thief

Sometimes the anxious alter ego makes us take on worries that aren't even our own. This makes everyone else's challenges our responsibility. For example, you might begin worrying about your parents' finances. "Can Mom and Dad pay for the house mortgage, and can they afford to buy me what I need?" Worries like that do not belong to you. They belong to your mom and dad, and you have to trust that they can take care of their own situation.

Or you may visit a doctor when you are sick, and even after she says you have just a mild cold, you continue to worry that your cold is actually the beginning sign of some rare disease! I mean, WebMD lists it as a possibility, so you should definitely be worried, right? No! You paid a doctor to use her expertise to diagnose you and tell you what's wrong and how to feel better. If you had a life-threatening illness, that would be your doctor's worry, and the doc would tell you that you also need to be worried. So if the expert isn't feeling worried, neither should you!

Take a moment to look back at your list of worries from Exercise 1 (page 26). Do any of the worries listed there belong to someone else? If so, it's time to let go of the worries that don't belong to you—and here's how:

Think about it. On some sticky notes or scraps of paper, write down each worry that doesn't belong to you.

Tear it. Rip up the pieces of paper, one by one, and tell yourself, "This is not my worry!"

Toss it! Send the scraps of paper into the recycling as you give yourself permission to let the worries go.

Trust others. Trust the people you care about, and trust the experts to handle their own worries and responsibilities.

QUIZ: *Help Out Matt*

Consider the following scenario: Matt is really afraid of heights. He is so afraid of heights that he has panic attacks when he drives over bridges, takes an elevator, or stands near windows on any floor higher than the first floor. Every time he even thinks about going somewhere above the ground level, he imagines that his knees go weak and he falls off the edge. He sees his car blasting off the edge of bridges and tumbling through the air. He sees elevator cords spontaneously snapping and the elevator he's in plummeting to the bottom of the building. These drastic, far-fetched images paralyze him and prevent him from enjoying many activities with his friends—no roller coasters or zip lines for Matt!

Take a look at each of the following situations that Matt encounters. Choose the tools that you think might help ease Matt's anxiety.

Situation 1:

Matt has to go to the doctor because he has a bad cold. Matt knows that to get to the doctor's office, his mom must drive over a long bridge. He's freaking out. What solution(s) will be best for Matt?

a. Convince his mom to change doctors.

b. Stay up all night thinking about how to make a parachute, just in case they fly off the bridge.

c. Use some quick math to determine the probability/chances of the car not making it safely over the bridge.

d. Stand up to his anxious alter ego. Tell the anxious alter ego that he will not be bullied into staying scared.

Situation 2:

Matt is going to an out-of-town soccer tournament with his soccer team. He is super excited to travel with his teammates. At the hotel, Matt realizes his room is on the 12th floor! YIKES! What solution(s) below will be best for Matt?

a. Ruminate about the elevator falling on the way to his room.

b. Put his thoughts on trial and come up with more realistic thoughts about his safety.

c. Take the stairs every time they come and go from the hotel.

d. Tell himself that disastrous elevator mayhem is the stuff of a great thriller movie, but not of real life! Instead, he should use that creativity to think about new soccer moves he can use to crush the other teams at the tournament.

Exercise 12: #NoFilter

You may wonder: "Why does my brain think this way?" "Where do these anxious thoughts come from?" Underneath most people's thoughts are **beliefs**. Beliefs are our deep-rooted understandings of ourselves and the world around us. We are not typically aware of these beliefs. Our brain just accepts them as true. Everyone has a handful of things that they deeply believe about themselves and the world; some of these beliefs are positive and some are negative. Here are examples of common core beliefs that are negative:

* I am not capable.

* The world is dangerous; I am not safe.

* I am not lovable.

* I am not good enough.

* I am worthless.

Think about beliefs as a filter you apply to a photo, like in social media apps. You take a selfie and then apply the filter. The original photo is the actual reality, but the filter that you see the photo through acts in a way that's similar to how core beliefs affect your thoughts about yourself, other people, and the world around you. Some core beliefs are positive and shape your perspective for the better, like adding a rainbow or a cool sunglasses filter to your photo. When your core beliefs are negative, the distortion is like a Snapchat lens that turns your face into a weird monster. But is this a true representation of you? Is that really who you are? NO! The anxious alter ego tries to use these negative filters so you can't see reality and you stay trapped in anxious cycles.

Here's an example of how core beliefs can filter our reality:

Situation: My biology teacher announces that there is a pop quiz.		
CORE BELIEFS	I am not good enough.	I am capable.
THOUGHTS	I'm going to fail! No way I can do this!	Oh, no! I didn't study, but I've been paying attention and doing my work. I can do this and will figure it out if there's something I don't know.
EMOTIONS	Anxiety Shame	Calm Confidence
ACTIONS	Panicked, mind goes blank, distracted	Deliberate, gives best effort, focused

Continued . . .

Exercise 12 Cont.: #NoFilter

Think of a time when you may have been influenced by negative core beliefs. Complete the chart by writing in the left column how the negative core belief affected your thoughts, emotions, and actions. How would things have been different if a positive core belief had been your filter? Write these outcomes in the right column.

Situation:		
CORE BELIEFS		
THOUGHTS		
EMOTIONS		
ACTIONS		

Exercise 13: **Shake Off Old Beliefs**

Core beliefs can be difficult to change for these reasons: (1) You aren't always aware of them, but they affect you every day, and (2) you have probably had these beliefs for years without knowing it. It's like breaking a habit that you've had for most of your life—not so easy! But once you realize what your core beliefs are, you'll start to see how they've been filtering your thoughts. It's like a light bulb turns on—"Hey, I didn't even realize I was sending myself that message!" Once you know what these beliefs are, you can begin to fight them off with positive self-talk and logic and by challenging old thinking habits.

What is one of your negative core beliefs?

_____

_____

_____

List evidence or information that proves this core belief is not accurate:

1. _____

_____

2. _____

_____

3. _____

_____

What is a more realistic belief you could have about yourself?

_____

_____

_____

Continued . . .

Exercise 13 Cont.: **Shake Off Old Beliefs**

List evidence or information that proves this belief is more realistic or true:

1. _____

   _____

2. _____

   _____

3. _____

   _____

Exercise 14: Judgment Day— in a Nice Way

Have you ever met someone who is super judgmental, constantly criticizing people for small, insignificant things? These people are usually not very pleasant to be around. Well, when highly anxious thoughts are in control of your thinking, you become that judgmental person, except that you are constantly criticizing yourself! The anxious alter ego tries to make you doubt yourself and believe that you cannot cope with difficult situations, compare yourself to others so that you feel less than, or assume things that are not true—which can leave you feeling self-conscious and helpless.

Generally, we are our own worst critics, yet we spend so much anxious energy on how we think others—friends, peers, teachers, coaches, parents, even random strangers—are judging us. That realization can help, but another way to combat unrealistic core beliefs and to be less judgmental of yourself is to know what makes you valuable. What are your strengths?

Take a moment to write down some of your strengths and values. What are the characteristics that you have that make you capable, that make you unique, and that give you strength?

_____

_____

_____

_____

_____

_____

_____

_____

_____

_____

_____

_____

_____

Continued . . .

Exercise 14 Cont.: **Judgment Day— in a Nice Way**

If you feel uncomfortable doing this, like you are bragging, let that worry go—you are simply stating the facts! It is important to practice focusing on your strengths and abilities, as your brain is probably used to doing the opposite. Here are some ideas for daily practice:

* Write positive and realistic statements about yourself on sticky notes. Post these notes where you will see them often, like your bathroom mirror, bedside table, desk, laptop, and notebooks.

* Take five minutes before bed each night to write down something you felt good about or accomplished that day.

* Set an alarm on your phone to go off once a day as a reminder to recognize how you were able to handle a difficult situation or to say something kind to yourself.

* Pair your favorite color with all your unique qualities and skills. *I love blue, and I am a loyal friend and family member. I am artistic. I stick up for others.* Or whatever it is for you. Then, throughout the day, when you see that color, let it remind you of who you really are and all that you are capable of.

* Follow social media feeds with confidence quotes and positive self-statements. Screenshot the ones that apply to you.

* Be creative—think of your own way to practice embracing yourself every day!

Exercise 15: Go Ahead, Make a Mistake!

It's the final two minutes of the basketball game, and you have to take the tie-breaking shot. You shoot. The ball swirls around the rim and bounces out.

It's been a long week, you're exhausted from working on so many projects, and you somehow forgot to bring your homework to class.

It's lunchtime. You are talking to your friends, and you stumble on your words.

All these scenarios are examples of mistakes people make every day. When you're experiencing high anxiety, however, these simple and normal mistakes feel like the end of the world. You think, *I've singlehandedly ruined the basketball team's chances for the playoffs. I'll never make it in college or be successful because I can't remember anything. I really can't talk! How clumsy I must look to everyone.* This is how anxiety makes us think about mistakes. It tells us that we aren't good enough, and that's why the mistakes happen. We think if we appear to be perfect, maybe no one will notice how terrible we really are. But as you are learning, anxiety does what? Yes, it LIES! It makes things feel worse than they are by sending us these negative, overblown messages.

The truth is that EVERYONE makes mistakes. EVERY DAY! Some mistakes are small, and, sure, some mistakes are kind of a big deal, but each and every mistake has a way that you can confidently deal with it. *You* get to decide how to move forward!

For example, after missing the last shot of the game, how could you handle this mistake?

a. Get angry and blame it on your teammates for not passing the ball to you soon enough.

b. Ridicule yourself for missing the shot, criticize your basketball skills, and consider quitting the team.

c. Tell yourself that it was a tough shot, work on that shot more during practice, and feel better prepared next time.

Mistakes and imperfections are critically important to learning. Mistakes teach us how to be braver, how to socialize, how to stand up for ourselves, and how to problem-solve. Try embracing mistakes and allowing yourself to make them with confidence.

Continued...

Exercise 15 Cont.: Go Ahead, Make a Mistake!

Think of a time when you made a mistake or felt imperfect:

What was the mistake?

_____

_____

_____

_____

_____

How did the mistake make you feel?

_____

_____

_____

_____

_____

How did you handle the mistake. What did you do?

_____

_____

_____

_____

_____

Was there anything you could have done differently?

_____

_____

_____

_____

_____

What could you have learned from the mistake?

_____

_____

_____

_____

_____

How would that have changed your emotions?

_____

_____

_____

_____

_____

TIP: Everyone makes mistakes, and nobody feels good about them. So the next time you see somebody in that situation, why not use your skills to help lift that person up? You could say something like "That was a really tough shot. Nice try." Or "I've struggled with that shot for years—we should practice together some time!" You're lifting someone up while reminding yourself that mistakes are okay—it's a win-win!

Exercise 16: Rumination Illumination

As we discussed in part 1, *rumination* is when you think over and over again about something that happened. Rumination is usually really unhelpful because it makes you focus on past negative events and keeps you stuck in an anxious cycle. But not all rumination is bad—sometimes, ruminating on an issue can shed light on how to solve the problem. Generally, thinking about past situations can be helpful if you are thinking about it to learn from it, find a solution, and move on.

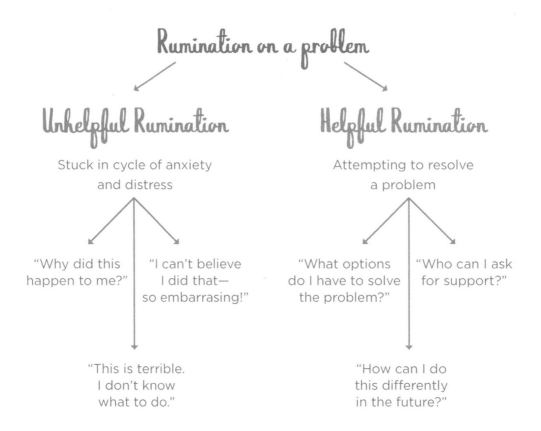

Helpful rumination focuses on thinking about an issue with the goal of solving it, acknowledging your ability to do so, and putting that plan into action. The rumination tends to stop after this. Rumination is unhelpful if...

* it increases your anxiety or causes you to dwell on the past.

* the questions you ask yourself focus on the cause of the problem rather than a solution.

Looking back at your anxious thoughts, are any of these thoughts that you dwell on? Has there been an issue in the past that you find yourself still focused on? Let's put those thoughts and issues to rest. Complete the following chart to practice problem-solving and releasing anxious thoughts.

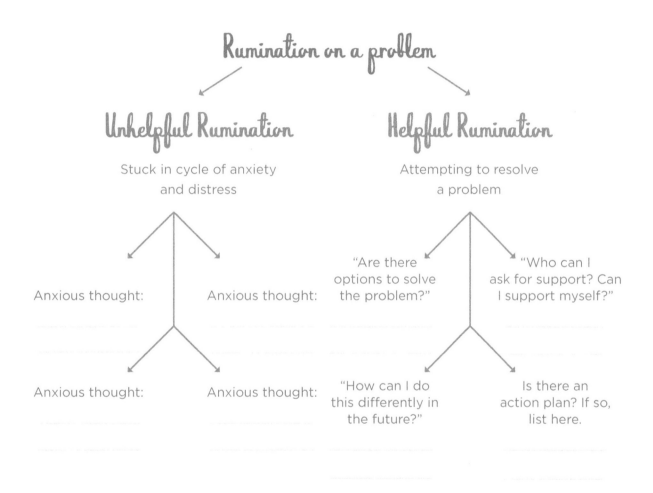

Rumination on a problem

Unhelpful Rumination

Stuck in cycle of anxiety
and distress

Anxious thought:

Anxious thought:

Anxious thought:

Anxious thought:

Helpful Rumination

Attempting to resolve
a problem

"Are there
options to solve
the problem?"

"Who can I
ask for support? Can
I support myself?"

"How can I do
this differently in
the future?"

Is there an
action plan? If so,
list here.

Continued . . .

Exercise 16 Cont.: Rumination Illumination

Do you feel any different after using helpful rumination? How do you feel now?

_____

_____

_____

_____

_____

_____

_____

_____

_____

_____

_____

_____

_____

_____

_____

_____

_____

_____

TIP: Sometimes the only solution to a lingering issue is to accept that it's over and move on. This is a good solution in itself. It tells us: There's nothing more to do on this one—you're older and wiser now, and it's time to let it go!

QUIZ: *What Would You Say?*

· ·

Using the skills discussed in Exercises 1 through 16, imagine your friend has the following problems. What would you say to encourage them and help them feel less anxious? What skills would you tell them to use?

1. Your friend wants to ask out someone but has been too scared to do it. They keep telling you that no one would want to date them.

What would you say to your friend?

_____

_____

_____

_____

2. Your friend says he is having trouble sleeping at night. He keeps thinking about someone breaking in. He can't stop his mind from thinking about all the bad things that could happen.

What would you say to your friend?

_____

_____

_____

_____

3. Two of your friends have been having an argument. One of them tells you that they are worried everyone will turn on them. They are obsessing about everything they have done to make their friends hate them.

What would you say to your friend?

_____

_____

_____

_____

Sometimes it's really hard to change our thinking for ourselves, but somehow it comes easily when we do it for others. Try being a friend to yourself. Think about what advice you would give your friend, and then try your best to apply it to yourself!

"You don't control me anymore"

Part Three

CALMING YOUR ANXIOUS BODY

One of the most difficult things about anxiety is that it's not only an emotional feeling; it's also a physical feeling. At its best, anxiety can feel like butterflies in the stomach or muscle tension, but at its worst, it can feel like you are dying! While you are actually completely safe from harm, the physical feelings you can get in your body are extremely uncomfortable and scary!

This section will teach you strategies for recognizing anxiety in your body, for learning to calm your body, and for staying in control when anxiety tries to take your body hostage.

Exercise 17: **Stress Balloon**

Stress, anxiety—what's the difference? These words are often used interchangeably because they can cause our bodies to feel very similar things. Stress and anxiety are different from each other, but stress can affect anxiety. Stress happens when you are dealing with pressures outside of yourself—it is *external*. For example, having a research paper due, hearing your parents fighting, or giving a speech to your class—these are stressful events. But usually the stress goes away after the event has passed. Anxiety, however, is a response to stress that you experience within you—it is *internal*. Anxiety typically sticks around even after a stressful event has passed.

If you have anxiety, knowing your stressors, or the things that stress you out, is important. The more stress you experience, the more difficult it is to manage your anxiety. Imagine that all the things that cause you stress are packed into a balloon. The more stress you have, the bigger the balloon gets. Eventually, the balloon overfills and . . . POP! You don't want to get to the point of popping, right? Managing the stress in your life will keep you from overwhelming yourself to that extent. Instead, begin to ask yourself, "Is this really worth being stressed about?" Reducing stress and things that trigger anxiety will make it much easier to control anxiety.

Take a moment to write down all the things in your life that cause you stress. Consider issues with school, family, friends, extracurricular activities, and so forth.

Now, ask yourself: Are there any of these that I can let go of? Which of these stressors have already passed by? Which of these are too far in the future? Which of these are out of my control?

Cross out the ones that you can release from your stress balloon.

Optional exercise: If you have a real balloon, go get it. After you have crossed out all the stressors that you can release, inflate the balloon while thinking of the stressors that remain on your list. Imagine that your breath is pushing those worries into the balloon, and that they no longer rest on your shoulders. Once the balloon is fully inflated (and nothing remains on your list), pop that stress balloon! Or, better yet, release the inflated balloon and let it fly all around the room, releasing your stressors into thin air. Bye-bye!

Exercise 18: **Sound the Alarm!**

When something really needs your attention, you are probably used to having some kind of alarm to let you know that you need to respond. When you need to get ready for school, you have an alarm that buzzes or sings or cock-a-doodle-doos until you wake up. When a chemistry experiment goes wrong at school, the fire alarm goes off, telling you to get outside as quickly as possible. Well, your body also sends you alarms to let you know when anxiety is about to take over and you need to do something about it. Those alarms are the physical feelings in your body. It's your body's way of communicating to you that it's time to use your skills to relax.

Here are some common physical feelings of anxiety that should signal an alarm for you to work toward feelings of calm:

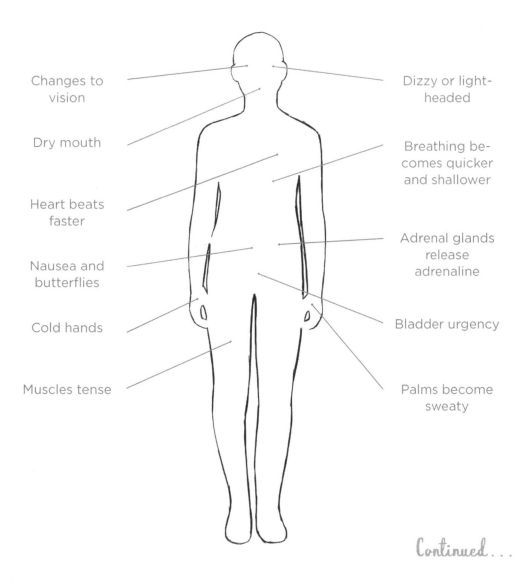

Changes to vision

Dry mouth

Heart beats faster

Nausea and butterflies

Cold hands

Muscles tense

Dizzy or light-headed

Breathing becomes quicker and shallower

Adrenal glands release adrenaline

Bladder urgency

Palms become sweaty

Continued...

Exercise 18 Cont.: **Sound the Alarm!**

In the picture below, circle the parts of the body where you experience anxiety. Do you feel it in your stomach, your shoulders, your forehead, your jaw—or somewhere else? Try to begin noticing these feelings in your body, and use them as a signal or alarm to try a relaxation skill or a thinking skill. Helpful skills include some of the exercises in part 3, such as **Take Time to Unwind** (page 70), **Breathe!** (page 75), **Mental Getaway** (page 77), and **Body Scan** (page 79).

Keep in mind: physical feelings of anxiety are not dangerous. A lot of people misinterpret their heart racing or breath changing as signs that they are dying or having a heart attack, but they're not! Your body was designed to go through these physical changes. Think about when you exercise. Your heart races, your breath gets shorter, you sweat. But you are confident that you are not dying. Physical responses to anxiety are similar; your body is just trying to get that anxious energy out.

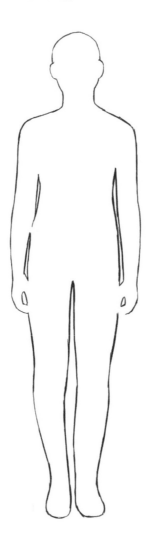

Exercise 19: What's My Emoji?

Checking in with your mind and body throughout the day is a great way to stay ahead of anxiety. Life can be so busy that most people don't realize the anxiety is building until it's too late and they're up to their necks in it. Knowing how anxious you are can help you identify if the anxiety is in that "just right" range that's beneficial to you, or if it's increasing and starting to cause you problems. Take a moment to check in now and rate your anxiety:

1   2   3   4   5   6   7   8   9   10

The best time to use an anxiety skill is when your rating is 3 or lower. This will help keep the anxiety manageable without ever letting it get out of control. However, you can always use skills when the number is higher, though it might require a bit more work and time because you have to come down from that anxious peak. You can also use skills when your number is zero. Just think about people who take time to meditate or do breathing exercises every day. Yes, some of these skills can become part of your daily routine, keeping you chill for longer and the anxious alter ego far away—so far that it may even face extinction in your world!

Exercise 20: **Take Time to Unwind**

Have you ever not been in the mood to do something but have to do that thing anyway? And afterward, you find yourself thinking, "I'm glad I did that!" And your mood seems better? Anxiety can often feel so overwhelming that you feel like you don't have the desire or energy to do something fun, relaxing, or distracting. But even if you aren't in the mood going into it, engaging in fun activities is so important for keeping anxiety away and your body healthy. Take some time to unwind!

Here are some examples of activities that you can add to your daily life, and also that you can turn to when you start to feel anxiety in your body or mind:

* Listen to music
* Bake something
* Play with pets
* Take a bath or a shower
* Watch TV or a movie
* Work out

* Do something artistic
* Take pictures
* Journal
* Call a friend
* Play video games

* Practice a sport
* Read
* Go for a walk or run
* Start a DIY project
* Dance

Make a go-to list of activities you enjoy that you can use to feel good and unwind. Get creative!

_____

_____

_____

_____

_____

_____

_____

Exercise 21: Stepping Up Self-Care

Believe it or not, the very basic things that you do every day, like sleeping, eating, showering, and so forth, are also important to help keep anxiety manageable. Check out these everyday tasks and tips for ways you can reduce anxiety by strengthening your daily self-care habits.

Sleep

Adequate sleep is crucial to your mental, physical, and emotional health. Believe it or not, a lot of activity goes on in your body while you sleep. Your brain and body recharge and even regenerate so you can function at your best each day. Imagine not charging your phone at night—it probably wouldn't last long the next day. Likewise, with insufficient sleep, you will be less able to concentrate, learn, perform necessary tasks, and cope with emotions. As a teen, you can find it extra challenging to get the right amount of sleep because you have so many demands on you in school as well as outside of school. Days are short, and you're so busy! It's especially challenging because research has shown that teens need at least 8 1/2 to 9 1/2 hours of sleep a night. Who's got time for that?

Kidding aside, even though it may not seem possible to get that much sleep each night, it's critical to your success. Research has shown that when adolescents increase their sleep, their grades improve, their SAT scores improve, their driving accidents decrease, and they can better manage their emotions. Here are some tips for improving your sleep:

* **Stick to a routine.** Try to go to bed and wake up at about the same time each day (even try to stick to it on weekends whenever possible!).

* **Use your bed only for sleep.** Your brain will start to associate your bed with sleep, and it will be easier to fall asleep. So take your homework, texting, and Netflixing elsewhere!

* **Go screen-free 30 minutes before bed.** Screens are a teen habit of epidemic proportions. So many teens fall asleep to the light of electronics, but guess what? Blue light and flashing images tell the brain it's time to be awake.

* **Establish a nighttime routine.** This routine tells the brain it's time to sleep. Your routine could be as simple as brushing your teeth, washing your face, throwing on jammies, and reading something light for 30 minutes. This will communicate to your brain that it's time to release the chemicals needed for sleep. For real—it's called melatonin!

* **Set up for cozy.** Make sure the temperature is right and your bed is comfy.

* **Prevent disruptions.** Turn off your ringer if possible. Use a white noise machine or fan to block out sounds that might disturb you.

Continued . . .

Exercise 21 Cont.: **Stepping Up Self-Care**

Nutrition

Eating and snacking throughout the day provides your body with the energy it needs to help you fight off anxious emotions and do your best at school, in social situations, and in your activities. Have you ever noticed how you get irritated or angry when you are super hungry (#hangry)? This is because emotions and nutrition are connected. Here are some tips for fending off anxiety:

* **Always eat breakfast.** Even if it's just a small bite or two.

* **Keep healthy snacks with you.** Good choices are nuts, trail mix, nutrition bars, or small bags of fruit and veggies.

* **Refuel when needed.** Try to snack when you start feeling tired or losing your ability to concentrate.

* **Focus on quality, not quantity.** Does your food have nutritional value? How's it helping your body refuel? Unfortunately, a soda and chips for lunch doesn't do the body much good beyond a quick sugar rush.

* **Water!** And more water! The benefits of water consumption on the body and brain are pretty incredible.

Hygiene

Showers, hot baths, brushing your teeth, splashing your face with water, brushing your hair, shaving, and so forth—these seem like simple tasks, and you may take them for granted. But these activities actually do wonders for relaxing and caring for your body, as well as for making you feel better about how you feel, look, and even smell! Make sure you take time to do them!

Activity

Getting active each day for at least 30 minutes is also important for managing your mood and taking care of your brain and body. This is another everyday activity that releases important hormones—in this case, endorphins—which are proven to make you feel good. Try making some activity a part of your daily routine. Here are some ideas:

* Take a walk
* Stretch
* Do yoga
* Play or practice a sport
* Lift weights
* Use an elliptical /treadmill
* Join an exercise class
* Dance
* Swim

We've covered sleep, nutrition, hygiene, and activity. Take a moment to consider how you can change or improve in each of these four areas. How are you inspired to kick-start a healthy everyday routine?

Sleep:

Nutrition:

Hygiene:

Activity:

Create a Self-Care Routine

Now that you know what self-care you do well and what areas could use some improvement, let's take a moment to create a daily routine. Use the following chart to plan how and when you will actually make these daily activities a real part of your life.

MONDAY				
TUESDAY				
WEDNESDAY				
THURSDAY				
FRIDAY				
SATURDAY				
SUNDAY				

TIP: Get creative and make your own schedule or routine in a bullet journal, digitally, or with any arts and crafts supplies you can find. Set self-care goals and check them off as you make progress. Make it unique and make it yours!

Exercise 22: **Breathe!**

"Just breathe!" It seems like overly simple advice we've all heard too many times, right? But actually this simple exercise is a proven strategy for keeping panic away. You may not have known this, but there are three different ways that people breathe: (1) relaxed breathing, (2) exercise breathing, and (3) anxious breathing.

* Relaxed breathing occurs when the body takes in oxygen and releases the same amount of carbon dioxide (CO_2). The oxygen and CO_2 levels are even. This balance allows the body to function well.

* Exercise breathing occurs when the body takes in more oxygen and simultaneously releases the same amount of CO_2. The additional oxygen allows the muscles of the body to perform the exercise. Because the body is exerting energy, the CO_2 output is also high. The oxygen and CO_2 levels are higher than in relaxed breathing, but the levels remain even.

* Anxious breathing occurs when your breathing increases so you take in more oxygen. But since the body isn't exerting any energy (because it isn't exercising), the extra oxygen doesn't get used up, and the body doesn't produce enough CO_2 to balance it out. The oxygen and CO_2 levels are not even. This imbalance causes many of the painful physical feelings of anxiety, including feelings of dizziness or lightheadedness, sweatiness, a racing heart, nausea, and shakiness.

The solution of course is to slow down your breathing. But how? Here's a breathing exercise to try:

* Slowly take a breath in through your NOSE to the count of 4.

* Hold your breath for 1 second.

* Slowly blow breath out through your MOUTH to the count of 6.

    (Your lips should be puckered as if you were about to give a kiss or blow a bubble.)

* Repeat this exercise three to five times. Each time, see if you can increase the count by one second more.

* Try to imagine calm blue air entering your lungs and anxious black air leaving your lungs.

Continued . . .

Exercise 22 Cont.: **Breathe!**

Try using this exercise at least once a day, even when you're not feeling anxious. If you teach your body how to do it when you are calm, then you are more likely to be able to slow your breathing when you're anxious. Practice, practice, practice—this is truly a proven method for calming down an anxious body!

TIP: Nervous during a presentation? Deep breaths can help, but here's another tool: Keep something in your hand that you can squeeze, touch, or focus on if needed. When you start to feel anxiety rise, try drawing your attention to the object in your hand (it can be notecards, a small stress ball, a hair tie, a pen, or something else) as you speak.

Exercise 23: **Mental Getaway**

When your mind is overwhelmed with racing thoughts about "What if this happens?" or "What if that happens?" it's time to harness that creativity into some what-ifs that actually reduce anxiety. You can do this by taking your mind on a little fantasy vacation. Yes, take your mind on a short trip somewhere soothing—which will give your brain a break, stop that anxious alter ego from snowballing out of control, and allow your physical body to regulate its breathing and release tension. Here's how you do it:

* If possible, close your eyes. If not, try picking a spot in the room that you can focus on.

* Use your five senses to imagine a scene of your choice. Where do you want to go? It can be a beach, an interstellar planet, a date with a celebrity crush, your favorite restaurant, a treasured vacation spot, and so forth. It can be somewhere you have been before, somewhere you wish to visit, or someplace completely imaginary!

* Sight: Focus on all that you can see in your imaginary scene with as much detail as possible. What's surrounding you? Who are the people with you? What are you wearing? What does your hair look like? What are the colors you see? Visualize as much as you can.

* Sound: What do you hear? Are you having a conversation? What are you saying? What are the background noises? Is music playing? Do you hear water lapping at the shoreline? Are birds singing? Are trees rustling in the breeze?

* Taste: Are you eating or drinking? What does it taste like?

* Touch: What do things feel like in your imaginary vacation? Do you feel the grains of sand between your toes on a beach? Or are you feeling the warmth of a fireplace at your favorite ski resort? Take as much time as you need to soak in all the feelings.

* Smell: What do your surroundings smell like? Salt from the beach air? Smoke from the fireplace? The perfume or cologne of your date?

Allow yourself to sink into your fantasized mental vacation. Visit your "places" on a regular basis. If your mind wanders back to anxious thoughts or even just to normal day-to-day thoughts, that's okay. As soon as you notice that your mind has wandered, bring it back to your mental getaway. This is like meditation. At first, your mind will wander a lot. The more you practice, the more your mind will be able to stay focused on your mental images. Who knew daydreaming could shrink anxiety? Bring it on!

Continued...

Exercise 23 Cont.: Mental Getaway

Jot down some ideas for mental vacations you'd like to take:

_____

_____

_____

_____

_____

_____

_____

_____

_____

_____

_____

_____

_____

_____

_____

_____

_____

_____

TIP: Try this at night when your mind won't turn off and you need some rest!

Exercise 24: **Body Scan**

Anxiety isn't just an emotional experience caused by outside forces; it lives in your body. It gets into your muscles, your stomach, your fingers, and your toes. Most of the time you don't really notice that your body is tensing up or that your muscles ache. You get used to carrying anxiety in your body and it becomes normal to you. Are your shoulders raised? Are your eyebrows set in a scowl? Is your neck tight? Is your jaw clenched? These are all signs of tension in the body. One way to get anxiety out of your mind is to get it out of your physical body first. This exercise will help you notice what an anxiously tense body feels like and to purposefully release that tension.

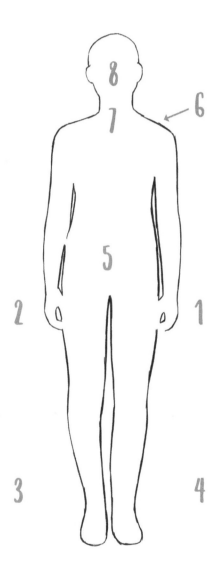

Continued . . .

Exercise 24 Cont.: **Body Scan**

TIP: When first trying out body scans (also known as progressive muscle relaxation), it can be helpful to use audio instruction. Some great options are available on YouTube. Try finding one that you like, with a voice and background that you find soothing. There are some very short ones for when you're in a rush and longer ones for when you have more time. See the Resources for Teens section (page 135) for links to helpful audio instructions.

To start your body scan, find a comfortable place to relax. You can be seated or lying down.

Start by thinking about your current anxiety level. At what number would you rate it (from 1 to 10)? _____

* Take three deep, slow breaths.

* Bring your attention to each of the parts of your body in sequence. Just take a moment to notice them, one by one, to see if you feel any tension or discomfort in each of them:

Right hand and arm	Left leg	Neck and throat
Left hand and arm	Stomach and chest	Face
Right leg	Back muscles and shoulders	

* Take another deep, relaxing breath.

* Now go through the sequence again. This time, tense up each part of your body as tightly as you can. Hold it for a few seconds. Notice what that tension feels like in your body. Now release the tension. Notice what it feels like when the tension leaves your body.

* Take another deep, relaxing breath.

* Go through the sequence again. This time, tense up each body part lightly (about half as much as the first time). Hold for a few seconds. Notice what that tension feels like in your body. Now release the tension. Notice what it feels like when the tension leaves your body.

* Take another deep, relaxing breath.

* Go through the sequence again. This time, notice if there is any tension left in each body part. Imagine any remaining tension leaving your body. Feel yourself sinking into the floor or chair. Imagine yourself getting heavier as your body relaxes more and more.

* Take three more deep, relaxing breaths.

How do you feel now? At what number would you rate your anxiety level? _____

You can use this exercise to help you notice what your body does when anxiety is creeping up. The more aware you are of what tension feels like in your body, the sooner you can act to keep anxiety from getting out of control.

TIP: Do body scans when you are feeling anxious—even covertly in public. How? Shorten the exercise up by doing just a few body parts, like your arms and legs. Make a fist and tighten and release. Curl your toes in your shoes, tighten, and release. And if you can, shrug your shoulders, then drop and relax them. It's unlikely that anyone will even notice!

Exercise 25: **Mindful Moment**

You now know how anxious thinking makes you think unrealistically. Another trick your anxious alter ego might use is focusing either on the past or the future. Does it dramatize and dwell on what happened in the past? Does it try to terrify you about unrealistic things happening in the future? If you can relate, get yourself out of this anxious cycle! How? By taking a bit of time each day to stay in the PRESENT.

Mindfulness is being aware of yourself and your environment in the present moment. Have you ever heard the saying "Stop and smell the roses"? Well, mindfulness has a similar meaning. It's all about taking the time to stop what you are doing and thinking, and home in on what's happening here and now. The goal is to reflect on the present moment without making any judgments or anxious conclusions about it. It can be hard to wrap your mind around the concept of mindfulness (excuse the pun)! The best way to understand it is to try some exercises. Here are a few:

* Look at one of your palms. Notice the lines in your hand. Notice the slight color variations in your palm. Notice the parts that are bony and the parts that are fleshy. Notice the different lengths of each of your fingers. Notice the unique prints on each of your fingertips. Notice any rings you are wearing. Take a finger from your opposite hand and trace along the lines of your hand as if they were all connected. Notice the sensations you feel.

What did it feel like to focus in on something intently for a few moments?

_____

_____

_____

How can you bring this same amount of focus to your everyday life?

_____

_____

_____

* Take a moment to notice the thoughts coming and going in your mind. Thoughts are just thoughts; they are not always worth paying attention to, and they are not always realistic. You can practice letting thoughts come and go without causing you any kind of big emotional response. Pretend your thoughts are like fireflies. As a thought comes to your mind, it lights up and glows for a few seconds. But then the thought passes, and the glow gets dimmer. Then another thought lights up and then dims. Acknowledge each firefly thought, and then allow it to dim and fly away.

Were you able to let your mind briefly focus on a thought without having anxiety creep in?

_____

_____

_____

* Wherever you are, stop and look around the room for a moment. Notice all the objects in the room. Notice objects that you are very familiar with, objects that you have looked at many times before. Now find a few things that you've never noticed before. What are some things you had overlooked or that you weren't aware of?

Are you surprised at how much you hadn't noticed before?

_____

_____

_____

Do you think there are other places or times in your life where you have been distracted and not aware of your surroundings?

_____

_____

_____

TIP: There are tons of amazing mindfulness apps and YouTube videos out there. These will guide you through lots of ways to practice mindfulness. Apps often have reminders to help you remember to practice. Most exercises take only one to five minutes of your time. But if you are really feeling overwhelmed, you may want to try a longer practice. See the Resources for Teens section (page 135) for apps and video suggestions.

Exercise 26: 5-4-3-2-1: You're Grounded!

No, this grounding is not when you get sent to your room and miss out on all the fun weekend activities! This grounding is similar to taking a mindful moment, and its goal is to get your head out of the clouds, reconnect with reality, and plant your feet back on the ground. Grounding can stop panic attacks and waves of intense anxiety by connecting your mind and body to your immediate surroundings. It gets you out of your anxious mind and into your safe surroundings. Here's how to do it:

5 sights: Take a look around. Choose five objects that you can see. Describe each of these objects to yourself in great detail.

* For example: I see a pillow. It is rectangular. It's about 18 inches by 10 inches. It has black, gray, and white colors. It has a zigzag pattern on the front and back. It has a zipper on the bottom. It looks like it's soft and fluffy. The gray fabric has flecks of lighter and darker colors. I can see the seam all around the pillow. It's leaning up against the cushion of a bench. (Do this for five sights.)

4 touches: Find four objects that you can touch. Describe the feeling of each of these objects to yourself in great detail.

* For example: I am touching my sweatpants. I can feel the supersoft cotton. I can feel the seam along the inside of the leg—it's a small line and ridged where the fold is. I can feel the elastic stretchiness of the waistband. I can feel the tie in the center. I can feel the fabric all the way down my leg. I can feel the different texture of the fabric around my ankle. (Do this for four touches.)

3 sounds: Find three sounds. Describe the sound of each of these objects to yourself in great detail.

* For example: I can hear the whirring of the air conditioner. It is making a very slight hissing sound as it blows through the vent. If I listen closely, I can hear a faint rattle coming from the somewhere in the wall as the air blows through it. (Do this for three sounds.)

2 smells: Find two smells. Describe the scent of each of these objects to yourself in great detail.

* For example: I smell the lotion I put on my hands this morning. It's a faint smell because most of it has faded, but I can still smell a little lavender. It smells fresh and clean. (Do this for two smells.)

1 taste: Find one item you can taste. Describe the taste of this item to yourself in great detail.

* For example: I can taste the water from my water bottle. It tastes light and clean. Not much flavor at all. If I swish it in my mouth, I can taste a slight mineral flavor. It is cool in my mouth and tastes refreshing. (Do this for one taste.)

By focusing in so much detail on the world around you and using all five of your senses, you can stop your brain from being able to focus on anything else. This buys you time for your body and mind to relax, and it stops the anxiety from building.

> TIP: If you don't have time to do the whole grounding exercise, try a shortened version. You can do one item from each of the five senses. Or just focus on sight and touch. Do as much as you can. The goal is to focus on as many details as possible so you distract yourself with peaceful, easy thoughts.

Exercise 27: Serene Space

Your mind is racing, your body is getting more tense, and everything around you seems loud and chaotic. You just need to escape for a short time! Even adults sometimes have to press pause on life and take a few moments to relax. Being able to call a time-out for yourself is a great skill to know. And having a place in your home or room where you can breathe and chill when you need to get away from it all can be super helpful. Here are some ideas for creating your own zen space:

Locate a cozy corner of your room, an unused closet, or an empty nook in a quiet place of your house.

* Make a tent—you're never too old to build a fort, and don't let anyone tell you otherwise!

* Set out a cozy pile of blankets and cushions and pillows.

* String up fairy lights or plug in a soft night-light to give some ambience.

Use aromatherapy

* Use an oil diffuser or spray to provide a calming scent.

* Lavender is known to be very relaxing, but use whatever scent speaks to you.

Include music

* Play some of your favorite music or relaxing sounds, like spa music.

Keep a little box or basket of de-stressing objects. These might include:

* Squishy toys/balls	* Bubble wrap	* Art pad and color pencils
* Silly Putty	* Adult coloring book	* Chewing gum or snacks
* Slime	* Journal	* Water bottles
* Brain teasers or puzzles	* Sticky notes	

What ideas do you have for your very own serene space?

_____

_____

_____

_____

Exercise 28: Avoiding Avoidance 1: a Little Science Experiment

Okay, so relaxing your body and hanging out in a cozy space are helpful and comforting activities you can do to keep anxiety more manageable. But sometimes you have to face the more difficult parts of kicking anxiety to the curb. When you get anxious, you're probably used to protecting yourself from that distress by avoiding everything that will trigger your anxiety. It's time to face the truth: The most powerful and effective way of getting rid of anxiety is to *not avoid it!* This is a habit that must be broken. And you can do this. Let's talk it through.

Every time you avoid a situation, your mind says to itself, "Aha! There really *is* something to be terrified of!" It's like you have a hypothesis about how things will turn out, but you never run the experiment to test the hypothesis. You just jump to the conclusion that your hypothesis is true. For example, you know social groups make you anxious. You worry you will say something stupid and that everyone will think you are weird and make fun of you. So when you get invited to hang out at the mall with a group of people, you turn down the invitation. By doing this you miss a chance to make stronger friendships, have fun, and build important social skills. Plus, who wants to hang out with their mom every single Saturday?

You jumped to the conclusion that you will make a fool of yourself, but no facts support that verdict. By turning down your friends' invitation to hang out, you told your brain there was truly something to fear. This avoidance tells the body to have an anxious response every time a social gathering occurs. So if you have a theory about how something will turn out, you have to test it. This is called "reality testing." You will be testing your expectations about how things will turn out so you can get at the truth or uncover reality.

So, let's do a science experiment. Think of a time when you avoided a situation because you were worried about the outcome. Complete the following chart for each time you need to test an anxious theory. Use the example chart to help you create your own:

Continued...

Avoiding Avoidance 1: a Little Science Experiment

Example Situation: Worried about hanging out at the mall with a group of people from school	
HYPOTHESIS What do you expect or predict will happen?	I will say or do something stupid. Everyone will think I am weird. I will be made fun of or talked about behind my back.
EMOTION How do you feel? How strongly do you feel this will happen (0–100%)?	Anxious Sad Self-conscious 95% certain it will happen
EXPERIMENT How could you test this prediction? What can you do if the thing you are worried about happens?	I guess I could go to the mall and try hanging out with them. If I say or do something stupid, I could just laugh it off or make fun of myself. If I act like I know it was silly, then maybe it won't be so bad.
OUTCOME What happened? Was your prediction true?	I went to the mall. I was really quiet at first, but I got more comfortable and started to talk more. I didn't really do anything weird. Everyone seemed pretty nice. My hypothesis was not true.
LEARNING What did you learn? What do you think will happen next time? How do you feel now?	Nothing terrible happened. Some of the people were cool. I might want to hang out with them again. I feel happy and a little less worried about how I am around groups of people.

Situation:	
HYPOTHESIS What do you expect or predict will happen?	
EMOTION How do you feel? How strongly do you feel this will happen (0–100%)?	
EXPERIMENT How could you test this prediction? What can you do if the thing you are worried about happens?	
OUTCOME What happened? Was your prediction true?	
LEARNING What did you learn? What do you think will happen next time? How do you feel now?	

Exercise 29: Avoiding Avoidance 2: Facing Fears

After reading the Specific Fears/Phobias section in part 1, did you discover that there is something specific you are afraid of? Spiders? Flying? The dark? Public speaking? Sleeping over at someone's house? If anxiety is preventing you from facing important activities or inevitable situations, one way to feel less anxious is to gradually face the very thing you fear. By facing the fear, you can learn that the worries in your mind are not going to happen. You also learn that even if things go wrong, you can handle it. This attitude communicates to the brain that you are a capable and confident person. As you know, avoidance is a short-term fix that only leads to more anxiety.

To really overcome your anxiety, you'll need to create a plan that slowly introduces you to what you are fearful of. Know that you will feel anxious, but by going slowly and using the skills you've learned throughout the book, the level of anxiety should be one that you can handle. Once you face the fear and the thing you are worried about does not happen, then each time you encounter it in the future, you will feel less and less anxiety.

Here is an example:

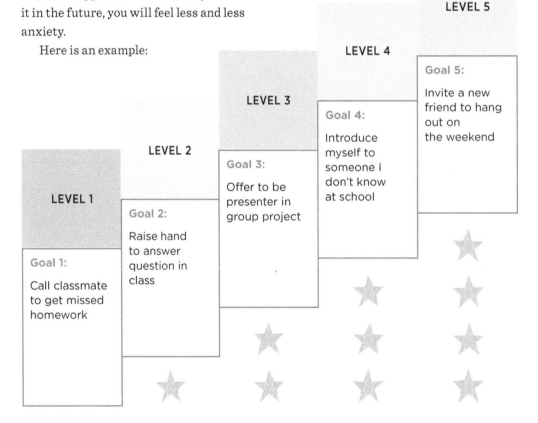

LEVEL 1

Goal 1:

Call classmate to get missed homework

LEVEL 2

Goal 2:

Raise hand to answer question in class

LEVEL 3

Goal 3:

Offer to be presenter in group project

LEVEL 4

Goal 4:

Introduce myself to someone I don't know at school

LEVEL 5

Goal 5:

Invite a new friend to hang out on the weekend

Think of this exercise like a video game. You'll start on an easy level, and as you work your way through, you will move up to more difficult tasks. But along the way, you'll be able to handle the more challenging levels because you will have acquired more skills, experience, confidence, and tools.

Think about a fear that you could gradually face and answer the questions below:

What is your feared situation? Try to be specific.

_____

_____

_____

_____

How could you gradually work toward facing that fear? How many levels of practice would it take?

_____

_____

_____

_____

What anxiety-reducing tools could you use at each level?

_____

_____

_____

_____

What rewards would help you stay motivated?

_____

_____

_____

_____

Continued . . .

Exercise 29 Cont.: Avoiding Avoidance 2: Facing Fears

With the information you just wrote down, create your own chart, with each level being a small goal you want to achieve. If you do not feel reduced anxiety at one of the levels, keep practicing at that level until your anxiety has reduced. Then move on to the next level. Just like in video games, you can't move on to the next level until you've mastered the level you are on!

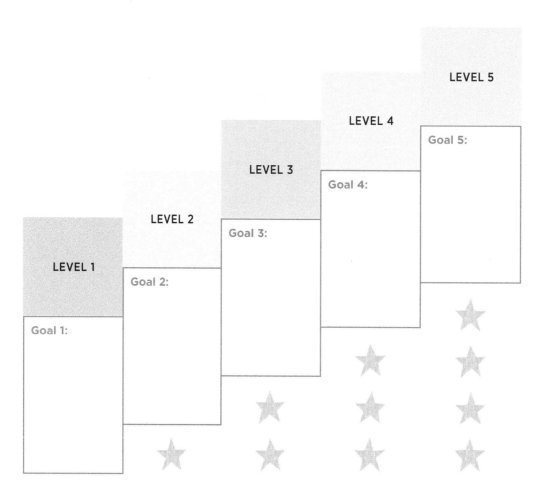

Exercise 30: **Treat Yourself**

Facing anxiety and practicing these tools is incredibly hard. And sometimes even finding the motivation to do it can be tough, especially when it can seem way easier just to avoid the whole mess altogether! But if you know ahead of time that you can provide motivation and celebrate your hard work, this can really help give you the push you may need. You *are* working hard and deserve to be rewarded!

The following are some ideas for things you can do to reward yourself. Some of them are small and simple, and some are a bit bigger for when you face more difficult challenges. Talk to your parents about which rewards they may be able to provide as well.

Experiences

* Go to a favorite restaurant
* Go to the movies
* Sleepover with friends
* Go to an amusement park
* Get a manicure/pedicure
* Go to a sports event
* At-home spa time
* Go to a concert

Privileges

* Later bedtime
* More screen time
* Access to car/driving
* Later curfew
* Chore pass
* More social time
* More game time
* Redecorate room

Objects

* Money for shopping
* Special item of clothing
* Jewelry
* Arts and crafts supplies
* Gas money
* Gift card
* New video game
* Money toward a large item

Continued . . .

Exercise 30 Cont.: **Treat Yourself**

What experiences, privileges, and objects would you like to use as motivation and reward? Choose from the items listed on page 93 or think of your own.

My reward ideas:

_____

_____

_____

_____

_____

_____

_____

_____

_____

_____

Exercise 31: **Being Assertive: A Balancing Act**

Assertiveness is when you firmly and clearly say what's on your mind in a respectful, kind way. You can think of it like a spectrum: being too passive is on one end, being too aggressive is on the other end, and being assertive is right in the middle.

Have you ever:

* felt really passionate about something but were too scared to speak up?

* felt like someone was walking all over you or taking advantage of you but didn't know how to stand up for yourself?

* needed something from someone but didn't know how to ask for it without sounding annoying or needy?

Speaking up and saying what you think or need can be really challenging, because you worry about what others will think: "Will they think I am too demanding, selfish, conceited, or aggressive?"

But by *not* communicating your thoughts and needs, a few negative consequences can happen:

* You end up being very passive, and people may take advantage of you.

* You push everything down until you explode. This is when you may come across as very aggressive and push people away.

* You send yourself the message that you are not worthy of getting what you need. This leads to low self-esteem.

* You send yourself the message that something bad will happen if you say what you need. This leads to more fear and anxiety.

To change this pattern, you'll want to practice being assertive.

Continued . . .

Exercise 31 Cont.: Being Assertive: A Balancing Act

Passive	Assertive	Aggressive
•Giving in to what everyone else wants •Not speaking up •Allowing yourself to be bullied •Thinking other people's needs are more important than yours •Consequence: Lower self-esteem •Consequence: Anxiety and fear •Consequence: Less respect from others	•Talking and listening equally, leading to compromises and solutions •Knowing that you matter just as much as everyone else •Looking for fairness in relationships •Standing up for yourself yet being respectful •Expressing your thoughts clearly and confidently •Consequence: Improves self-esteem and reduces anxiety •Consequence: Builds healthier relationships	•Acting like your needs are more important than others •Talking over or not listening to others •Demanding that things always go your way •Bullying •Shouting or getting physically aggressive •Consequence: Pushes people away •Consequence: Hurts self-esteem of others

Take this scenario, for example:

Shauna and Emily are best friends and do everything together. Emily makes most of the decisions about what they are going to do for fun, where they will go to eat, and what movies they will see. Shauna is pretty laid back and usually doesn't mind, but sometimes she wishes she could share her input. One day Emily tells Shauna that Shauna can't hang out with a girl named Ashley because Emily doesn't like her. Shauna has only had positive experiences with Ashley and thinks Ashley is really nice. She wants to be friends with Ashley too, but she is worried Emily will be angry and stop being her friend.

*If Shauna were to proceed too **passively**, here is how that might play out:*

Shauna stops talking to Ashley. She never tells Emily how she feels. Every time Emily talks trash about Ashley behind her back, Shauna goes along with it and laughs. Inside, Shauna feels really bad, but she just keeps her thoughts to herself. Emily continues to boss Shauna around and eventually gets annoyed that she always has to make the decisions and finds Shauna to be too dependent and weak.

*If Shauna were to proceed **aggressively**, here is how that might play out:*

Shauna finally has it with Emily always telling her what to do! She yells at Emily and tells her that she is bossy and demanding. She tells Emily that she can't stand it anymore and no longer wants to be friends. She hangs out with Ashley instead and starts gossiping about Emily. She spreads rumors about Emily to get others to stop hanging out with her, too. Emily feels terrible and lonely and hurt that everyone seems to be against her.

*If Shauna were to proceed **assertively**, here is how that might play out:*

Shauna tells Emily that she totally understands that Emily doesn't connect with Ashley and that they won't be friends. But Shauna tells Emily that she likes Ashley and wants to give a friendship with her a shot. She tells Emily that she hopes she understands and promises that it won't get in the way of their friendship. Emily is disappointed but says okay. Shauna also starts telling Emily when she wants to do something different, like go to her favorite restaurant. Sometimes they disagree, but when that happens they work to find a compromise.

Here are some tips for being more assertive in those situations:

1. **Look confident.** Make eye contact, stand up straight, and speak clearly and calmly.

2. **Stay cool.** Keep your emotions in check and stay calm and levelheaded.

3. **Be clear.** Specify what you need or want. Use "I statements," such as:

   "I don't want to talk badly about people behind their backs."

4. **Be candid.** Tell others how their actions are making you feel, such as:

   "When you interrupt me or talk over me, I really feel like you don't care about what I have to say."

5. **Be respectful but firm.** Acknowledge how the other person must feel, but still state your perspective. See if there is room for compromise. Try this:

   "I know you love horror films, but they give me nightmares. I just can't watch that one. What other movies would you be willing to see?"

Can you think of a time when you felt like you were being too passive or aggressive? Take a moment to write down how you could have been more assertive.

_____

_____

_____

"I know what you mean"

Part Four

PUTTING YOUR TOOLS TO WORK Q&A

Now that you've explored all the tools and exercises that can keep anxiety manageable in your mind and your body, it's time to see how to actually use them in real life. In this section, we'll walk through some real scenarios that teens face frequently. You will see how the exercises can help with everyday problems. We'll highlight a few exercises for each problem, but keep in mind that you can use any number of tools in this book for each problem. By practicing and understanding what your anxiety is like, you can start to narrow down the exercises that work best for you!

Q: I have to present my project to my entire class. What if I have anxiety or a panic attack while I'm standing in front of the class?

A: *To manage anxiety in a situation like this, here are a few steps you can take:*

1. Practice. Practice alone, and then practice in front of others if you can. The more you practice, the more prepared you will feel, and this should reduce some of the anxiety.

2. **Do the Math** (page 40):

    How many panic attacks have you had while presenting before?

    How many other people have panic attacks during presentations?

    How likely is it that it will happen to you?

3. Do the **Worst-Case Scenario** exercise (page 37):

    If a panic attack does happen during your presentation, what's the worst that could happen? That you have symptoms that are very uncomfortable and you have to stop the presentation?

    Okay, so how would you handle it? What would you do? Ask to finish the presentation later? Go to bathroom to get yourself calm? Make a joke out of it to the class and try again? Take a poor grade now, but discuss your concerns with your teacher after class? You have options, and none of them result in the end of the world!

4. Remember the **Imaginary Audience** (page 8):

    Everyone believes that they are on stage and being judged. This means that just like you, everyone in the class is terrified about giving a speech and worried about how they will appear.

    Your classmates are probably so distracted by their own worries about their performance that they are barely paying attention to you!

    When you feel symptoms of anxiety, like feeling hot, shaky, or flushed, remember that usually you are the only one who will notice them. No one else can really tell.

5. Relax your mind and body:

  Before and during the presentation, **Breathe!** (page 75). Take several deep, slow breaths before you begin, to keep panic symptoms to a minimum. During your presentation, take your time and find places where you can pause to take a deep breath.

  Remember my tip (page 76) to hold something in your hand that you can focus on if needed. When you feel anxious, shift your attention to the object in your hand. Keep going with your presentation as you also focus on the feeling of what's in your hand.

Q: I have a crush on someone, and I know they don't like me back. If they find out I like them, they will definitely laugh at me and think I'm stupid. I just can't face the rejection. I'm going to have to avoid them in the halls and see if I can switch out of the classes that we have together.

A: *Having a crush can be really hard! You may feel really vulnerable and scared that they won't return your feelings. Here are some things to consider:*

1. Are you using any Thinking Errors (page 30)? Thoughts like "I know they don't like me back," and "They will *definitely* laugh at me," are probably the thinking errors caused by *Jumping to Conclusions*. You assume you know what your crush is thinking, and you are predicting the outcome. As great as you are, you are not psychic! You cannot read people's minds or see the future, so don't go beating yourself up with self-destructive thoughts that may be very far from the truth.

2. Consider some Gray Thoughts (page 43). Are there any other explanations or possible outcomes here? Is there a chance that your crush may like you back? Or even if they aren't into you romantically, maybe they still think you're cool? Or if they don't like you at all, maybe they suck and have really bad taste?

3. Avoiding Avoidance 1: a Little Science Experiment (pages 87–92)! Avoiding stressful situations communicates to your brain that your negative thoughts are right: that you will be rejected and that you won't be able to handle it. So, instead, don't avoid your crush. Continue on as you normally would, and even dare to say hi! Prove to yourself that nothing bad will happen, that even if your crush isn't into you, you can still go to class with them and be your awesome self.

Q: Alex unfollowed me on social media. Should I delete my account? It feels like everyone hates me.

A: *Social media is amazing and addictive, but not always in a good way! Sure, it's easy to get lost in the feeds. But it can also be a place where you end up overanalyzing yourself and everything you post. If you encounter a social media diss, try this:*

1. Put your phone somewhere far away. Go to your Serene Space (page 86). Spend a little while relaxing in a place that brings you calm and makes you feel safe.

2. While you're in your serene space, take another look at the #NoFilter (page 50) and Shake Off Old Beliefs (page 53) exercises. Are you possibly looking at this situation with a negative filter (thoughts like "I'm not likable")? Is anxiety making you put yourself down and believe that everyone else is, too? Try using the Shake Off Old Beliefs exercise to stand up to these anxious beliefs, and to identify a more realistic thing to believe about yourself, like "I'm pretty awesome, and I'm well liked by some great people!"

3. Work on Taking Charge of Your Anxious Alter Ego (page 28)! Tell that anxious jerk, "Not everyone has to 'like' me. And I don't have to like everyone. If someone doesn't want to follow me, that's cool, and it's their loss."

Q: Sarah is so cool, and she's so pretty. She has hundreds of followers on social media, and it seems like the whole school loves her. I feel envious of her perfect life. I am such a loser; I'll never be like her.

A: *Sarah does sound like she's got it all. But do you think her life is really so perfect ALL of the time? Is she really without flaws? Here are some things to consider:*

1. Check your thoughts. Seems like there might be some Thinking Errors (page 30) here. Like overgeneralizing. Does the whole school really love her? Does she really have a perfect life? And maybe you are negatively labeling—calling yourself a loser? I suspect that there is some distortion in how you are viewing both yourself and Sarah.

2. If you find that you are often putting yourself down and comparing yourself to others, take a moment to reflect on yourself and your strengths, your value, and everything unique about you that makes you who you are. Check out the Judgment Day—in a Nice Way exercise (page 55). Try using one of the activities to see why you are just as valuable as everyone else, even the all-amazing Sarah!

Q: I'm so tense and stressed. I can't sleep, so I stay up all night on my phone.

A: *It's so frustrating that when you lie down to rest, all the anxious and stressful thoughts rush in to your brain! The phone can really help distract, but it will also keep you from getting to sleep. The light and the language that come from the phone send signals to your brain that you need to remain alert. By not getting enough sleep, both you and your phone will have dead batteries, and you won't be able to handle the very things you were stressed about. Instead of relying on your phone to chill you out, try out one or two of these exercises to help you relax your mind:*

1. Take a look at the Stepping Up Self-Care exercise (page 71). How does your sleep measure up? Are there any things you could do differently to help yourself out at night?

2. If your mind begins to race when you are trying to go to sleep, the Mental Getaway exercise (page 77) could be really helpful for you. This exercise will focus your mind on something relaxing. Your brain will struggle to think about both your mental getaway and your daily stressors. By shifting your brain to focus only on the mental getaway, your brain and body will begin to relax and drift off to sleep. Remember, it might be hard to keep your focus on your imagery at first, but the more you practice, the easier it will become. Be patient and give your brain time to learn this new skill.

Q: Caleb said yesterday that I suck. He said he was joking, but it really hurt my feelings.

A: *Sometimes even our friends say and do things that hurt us. This simple jab may have not been on purpose to hurt you, but if it did, it's important to understand why and to talk it through with your friend. Consider these points:*

1. Why do you think this bothered you so much? Strong emotions are signals that something is going on outside your awareness that you might want to tap in to. Maybe when your friend jokingly said "you suck," it triggered your core belief filter, that somewhere deep inside you, sometimes you say "you suck" to yourself, and when your friend said it, it hurt because it compounded your negative feelings. But the reality is, that core belief isn't accurate. Take a look back at the #NoFilter (page 50) and Shake Off Old Beliefs (page 53) exercises to test this theory out.

2. If something a friend is doing is triggering negative feelings for you, it's okay to ask them to stop. Use the Being Assertive exercise (page 95) to come up with ideas for something you can say in response. Remember, it's not mean or selfish to ask for what you need! Be respectful and kind, but be clear and confident in your request. Perhaps say something like, "I know you were just joking around, but I really don't like it when you say things like that. Please don't say I suck anymore. Thanks, man." If your friend is a good friend, they will not have a problem with it.

Q: I have a baseball game this weekend. What if I strike out and we lose? It will be my fault, and I'll be benched or kicked off the team—and my teammates will be mad at me!

A: *The pressure of team sports is insane! It can feel like everyone is relying on you, and of course you want to do well and make a good impression on your teammates, coaches, and everyone watching. But sometimes that pressure gets blown out of proportion. The anxious alter ego makes us fear some pretty outlandish consequences. Let's break this anxious thinking down:*

1. Let's check whether there are any Thinking Errors (page 30) here. Looks like you may be using the *Personalization* error by taking all the blame for an outcome on yourself. Baseball is a team sport, and no one person can be held fully responsible for how the game turns out. Try owning only your part, and recognize that others participated as well.

2. It's hard to tell if you should really be worried that your teammates will be super angry or if you will be kicked off the team. One way to decide if you need to be worried or chill is to put your Thoughts on Trial (page 35)—take a look back at that exercise. Your worry thought is that you will make a mistake so big that it will result in your being kicked off the team and angering your teammates. What evidence do you have to support this drastic outcome? Is it common for people to be kicked off the baseball team when they don't perform perfectly? Are your teammates really that easily angered, or are they generally supportive? Would they be mad that they lost as a team or would they be mad specifically at you? Also, think through the evidence that shows this feared outcome is not realistic. When this kind of thing has happened before, what actually resulted? If a mistake did occur, what different ways could you handle it? Take a look at all the evidence and decide how worried you should be. Then come up with a more realistic statement like "I can't be perfect during this game, but I can do my best, support my team, and try to learn something that will make me better for the next game."

Q: Am I the reason my parents fight? Are they going to separate because of me?

A: It's normal for parents to fight sometimes. Sometimes it's no biggie and they will make up and move on, and sometimes they have bigger problems that they are working on. But 100 percent of the time it is not your fault. Your parents are adults who must figure out what is best for themselves, both in their relationship and in taking care of their own needs. Try not to be a Worry Thief *(page 48). Their worries about how to take care of their relationship is not your worry; that is, you have no control over the outcome. Trust that they know what they are doing and that you are safe and loved, no matter what they are up to. Here are some other things to try:*

1. Try Being Assertive (page 95). If you hear your parents argue or fight, let them know how it makes you feel and respectfully ask that they not fight in front of you. Here's an example: "I know it's normal for parents to fight sometimes, but when you do it in front of me, or when I can hear it, it really worries me. Can you guys please try not to do that?"

2. Try doing something that relaxes you to keep the anxiety of parent worries away. What fun activities or distractions can you come up with in the Take Time to Unwind exercise (page 70)?

Q: I'm behind on all my assignments. What if I fail?

A: *Sometimes it feels like all the school assignments, projects, and tests hit at once! And why do some teachers think their class is the only one that matters? Don't they know you have other classes, too? In this situation, consider trying the following:*

Remember the Keeping It Real exercise (page 45)? Well, admittedly, this is one of those times when you are probably not going to be super positive. It would be unrealistic to say that this is going to be an "awesome week" or "I'm so perfect and amazing, I won't have any trouble getting this done." While you are amazing, this situation would be tough for anyone! But it's also just as unrealistic to think about this situation with total negativity like "There is no way I can do all this" or "I'm stupid and can never stay ahead." In the moment you may feel helpless, but it just simply isn't so. What would be a more "real" way of talking to yourself that might actually help you ease your anxiety and make some progress? How about saying, "This is a crappy week and I'm not sure everything will be done perfectly, but if I put my worries aside and just work on a different subject each night, I'll probably get it done." And you could say, "If it doesn't all get done, I'm going to speak with my teachers and see what my options are. They're more likely to help if they know I am working at it and proactively problem-solving with them." In your own words, what realistic statements would you make in this situation?

Q: I really want to go to summer camp this year with all my friends. But I can't sleep when I'm away from home for a whole week. I'm terrified I will be homesick in front of everyone and not have fun.

A: *Being out of your comfort zone for the first time is the perfect situation for the anxious alter ego to creep in and cause all kinds of chaos in your mind. But you can fight back against these anxious tricks. Here's how:*

1. Build confidence in your ability to handle these kinds of new situations by using the Avoiding Avoidance 2: Facing Fears strategy (page 90). One level at a time, you'll work to reach the goal of feeling more confident about sleeping away from home. It might look something like this:

   Level 1: Do a mock campout at your own home. Pitch tents in the backyard and invite several friends over. Do the whole s'mores thing. Plan some outdoor camplike activities. And if your parents are cool with it, have a firepit and tell camp stories.

   Level 2: Spend the night away from home with someone you feel very comfortable with, maybe a best friend or a close family member, such as your aunt and uncle or grandparents.

   Level 3: Spend an entire weekend away from home with someone you feel very comfortable with, such as a best friend or family member.

   Level 4: Spend one night away from home at a friend's house where you haven't spent much time.

   Level 5: Spend a weekend away from home at a friend's house where you haven't spent much time.

   Level 6: See if your parents will let you do a mock campout away from home, like at a nearby campsite or lake. Invite several friends. Pretend you are already at your summer camp. Have your parents set up camp at a nearby campsite.

   Note: It's okay to repeat each level until you feel like your anxiety is under control. Then move on to the next level.

2. At each level, think of how you can Treat Yourself (page 93) for your hard work along the way. Remember, you are trying something new and pushing yourself to be brave in a new experience—that's amazing work, and you deserve to reward yourself for trying!

3. At each level, bring a few things from home that give you comfort, such as a favorite blanket or pillow. And think about what tools you can use from this book to defeat the anxious alter ego, like one or more of the following:

   - 5-4-3-2-1: You're Grounded! (page 84)

   - Body Scan (page 79)

   - What Would You Say? (page 63)

   - Do the Math (page 40)

   - Mental Getaway (page 77)

   - Take Time to Unwind (page 70)

4. Some more things to remember:

   - Homesickness is completely normal, especially the first time or two you are away.

   - When you go away, you may notice that homesickness dwindles over time, especially if you stay busy and engaged in conversation. Being alone or without activities gives your brain more time to focus on anxious thoughts.

   - Don't let anxiety rob you of having fun with your friends and trying out new experiences! It's okay to be a little anxious because this is new, but try to focus your attention on all the things you want to do while at camp.

   - You will be home soon. This is not forever! And just think of all the great stories you'll have to share with your family!

Q: I have a major term paper due, and I'm so worried that I won't finish on time. I can't stop thinking about it!

A: *Big projects, tests, performances—they can all cause your mind and body to feel anxiety and a sense of doom that they won't get done. You may feel like there's not enough time, and of course your brain just doesn't want to cooperate! But dwelling on the problem is not helpful. It doesn't give you more time, it doesn't give you a solution, and it doesn't make you feel calmer. Try spinning things in a more positive way with the* Rumination Illumination *exercise (page 60). If you are going to spend time thinking about it, why not think about it in a way that helps you solve the issue and move on? To ruminate in a more helpful way, ask yourself* how *and* what *questions. Avoid asking* why *questions. Something like this:*

* How much time do I have before this paper is due?

* How can I divide up what is left across each hour or day?

* What other options do I have to help me get this done?

* Where can I work that will help me focus the best?

* Is there anyone I can ask for help?

* What are my options if I'm not able to finish on time?

* How can I plan differently for the next paper?

* What can I take away from this experience?

Q: I had a panic attack yesterday. It was the worst feeling ever! I am so scared that it will happen again, I don't even want to leave my room.

A: Panic attacks are the worst! They're so uncomfortable and can really feel like something terrifying is happening to you. As hard as it sounds, the way to ease panic in the moment is to do everything you can to keep your body calm and your mind focused on safety. It's your anxious alter ego that wants your body to go into fight-or-flight mode and is tricking your mind into thinking you're in danger. But you can fight these urges with practice. Try this:

1. Practice paying attention to your body. Knowing what your body feels like when anxiety is approaching can help you get calmer sooner and hopefully stop a panic attack before it happens. Take a look at the Sound the Alarm! exercise (page 67) to identify where anxiety shows up in your body. The moment you notice tension or discomfort in these areas, use that as a signal to start some relaxation exercises.

2. With a panic attack, the first thing to always focus on is getting your breathing under control. This will have a positive domino effect on all the other sensations you may be feeling. Look back to the Breathe! exercise (page 75) and explore the ways to slow your breathing. Take in slow, deep breaths from your nose and blow even slower out of your mouth. Keep doing this while you try the exercise in step 3.

3. In the 5-4-3-2-1: You're Grounded exercise (page 84), you can distract your brain from fearful thoughts and stop your brain from focusing on how the panic is making your body feel. Use all your attention to think in detail about the things you see, touch, hear, smell, and taste.

4. If your mind wanders to your worries, try reciting this message to yourself (you can also have this on a notecard and keep it in your purse, wallet, or backpack):

    I'm not in danger. I am safe.

    The worst of these feelings will pass in 10 minutes or less.

    I can handle 10 minutes of this discomfort.

    I have survived this before.

    I can help myself get calm.

Don't avoid life. Staying home or in your room will not keep panic attacks away—in fact, it will only increase anxiety and unnecessary fear. Do not let panic attacks chain you down. You have the power here—use your tools to help you.

Q: I completely forgot about my algebra homework! I am in such a panic, I can't believe I could be so stupid! What am I going to do? My teacher is going to be so angry.

A: *Yep, forgetting your algebra homework one time is definitely the worst thing you could do; you're the worst! Just kidding, that was reverse psychology! Messing up, forgetting, or just completely spacing out may seem like a huge mishap, but it's completely normal! Literally everyone does it—a lot! What is important to work on is changing how you talk to yourself when these completely normal things happen. Here are some things to try:*

1. Review the **Go Ahead, Make a Mistake!** exercise (page 57). Remember that mistakes are a part of life. They will happen over and over again. It's okay to make them! They will make you stronger, braver, smarter, and more capable when the next big challenge comes your way.

2. You aren't perfect, and you shouldn't strive to be. Instead, focus on being a good problem solver and dealing well when mistakes do happen. So in this situation, how could you solve the problem? Try this:

    - Accept that you forgot your homework. Tell yourself that you are okay, and that it happens.

    - Think about a solution: Is there a way you can get it done quickly before class? Can you talk to your teacher and arrange to make it up? Can you turn it in tomorrow and accept a late grade? If you take a late grade, can you do some extra credit work at another time?

Watch how you talk to yourself. Mistakes do not make you stupid, bad, incapable, or less than. Mistakes can even make you stronger and wiser. When mistakes happen, talk to yourself the way you would talk to a friend. You would never tell your best friend that they are stupid for forgetting their homework!

Q: I walk into the gym for an assembly, and I swear everyone is looking at me. This big group of popular kids just busts out laughing. They must be making fun of me—maybe they think I'm weird or something! Where should I sit? Everyone will think I'm stupid if I try to sit next to them.

A: *Remember that whole* Imaginary Audience *thing (page 8)? Well, this annoyingly shows up a lot in the teenage years. It'll make you feel like you're on stage doing the most ridiculously embarrassing things of your life, and everyone is watching you and judging you. But, in reality, all the other teenagers are on their own stage worried about what everyone is thinking about them. Even the most popular, seemingly perfect kids in school feel the effects of the imaginary audience phenomenon—they worry, too. When self-conscious thoughts pop into your mind, try the* Fake News *exercises (page 47):*

1. Let thoughts just be thoughts. Obviously, every thought that enters your mind is NOT true. Practice telling yourself, "These are just thoughts. It doesn't mean they are true!"

2. Spin your creativity differently. Instead of imagining everyone is laughing at you, try to imagine a different reason they are laughing. Maybe one of them burped really loud and everyone is laughing. Maybe they're all sugar-crazed and giggly because they had too much soda and candy at lunch. And, frankly, the entire school is in the gym. What are the chances that all of these hundreds of kids sitting there, they are laughing at YOU?

3. Let it go. Remember, every thought isn't worth your time and attention, so start practicing letting some of the thoughts pass through you. Pick up the remote control in your mind and hit the Next button. Keep clicking through thoughts until you land on one that makes you feel good, just like scanning though Netflix series or channels on the television.

Q: My friends have started drinking. They keep asking me if I want to, but I don't think I do. I'm worried that if I say no, they will stop hanging out with me.

A: *It is so hard when your friends start doing things you're not sure about. You want to be included, but you also want to do what feels right to you. It feels like you are stuck in the middle of two wrong decisions. Even though it seems that way, it usually ends up okay, and true friends are usually understanding. Here are some things to consider:*

1. Most friends will respect your choices, but you have to vocalize them. If you never speak up, they'll make assumptions and may unintentionally pressure you, not realizing you're against it. If they know your stance, they're more likely to respect it, even if they lovingly poke fun at you a bit. Take a look at the Being Assertive exercise (page 95) to see ways that you can communicate your limits with them. It may sound something like "I know you want to drink and whatever, but I'm just not into it right now. I'll be the designated driver if you get in a jam—just don't be too hungover for our lacrosse game tomorrow [or the video game marathon, or fill in your favorite sober activity here _____]!"

2. This is tough, but if you know that one of your friends is not okay with you being yourself and doing what you want to do for you, then it's probably time to reevaluate the friendship. How does this friendship benefit you? Have you grown apart? Is it time to move on and appreciate the friendship for what it was when it was healthy in the past? Saying goodbye to a friendship is never easy, but sometimes it can be for the best. Take some time to evaluate if this option is for you. Look, you can always say "hi" and be respectful—you're just not hanging out with the person anymore. And sometimes these friendships come full circle, once everyone's matured a little and outgrown their wild or reckless phase.

Q: I just feel so anxious all the time. My stomach hurts, my muscles hurt. The worst part is, I don't even know what I am anxious about!

A: *Anxiety can physically hurt! It can cause your muscles to tense up and cause stomachaches, headaches, skin rashes, and more. Thankfully, while these things hurt and are super uncomfortable, they aren't anything that could seriously hurt you. You are a young, healthy teenager, so don't confuse anxious tension with having a serious medical problem. That said, you don't want to feel this way, and I don't blame you! This is your body communicating to you that you are anxious and need to do something to relax. Remember the* Sound the Alarm! *exercise (page 67)? Knowing your body's signals that you are getting anxious will help you take action earlier, which will keep the anxiety at a manageable level. When you feel anxious tension in your body, go to your* Serene Space *(page 86) and try one of these ways to relax:*

1. Check out the Body Scan exercise (page 79). You can even pull up a YouTube video or sound clip of a body scan (see the Resources for Teens section for links, page 135). Guide yourself through each muscle group in your body as you purposefully release the tension from your body. Remember to breathe slowly to get just the right amount of oxygen to each of your muscles (see Breathe! on page 75). Slow, deep breathing will help loosen the tension throughout your body. Try to think of your muscles as being like spaghetti noodles. They are like uncooked, hardened noodles when you're carrying anxiety, but by the end of the body scan, you've released the tension, and your muscles should feel like cooked noodles, limp and flexible.

2. If your body is building anxious tension, it probably means that your mind is off doing too much thinking about something—either something that happened in the past or something that may or may not happen in the future. This type of thinking can happen without your even being aware of it! Try taking a mindful moment. By giving yourself a little time each day to focus in on the present moment, the chaos of your mind and body will slow down. Try one of the activities from the Mindful Moment exercise (page 82) to find some calm, or check out the link to the Six-Minute Mindful Moment (page 136).

Q: I don't know if I can take the pressure anymore! I have soccer practice before school, games on weekends, theater after school, performances all the time, plus I'm taking four advanced classes, volunteering for community service hours, and working as a youth leader at youth group! I don't have any time to spend with my friends, and I'm tired all the time.

A: WOW! How could anyone keep up with all those demands? Remember the Stress Balloon exercise (page 66)? While individually each of these activities is important and fun to you, by having to do them all at once, they are becoming sources of stress. When we have too many stressors at once, our stress balloon is likely to pop! You may be thinking, "But I need all these activities on my college application to stand apart!" or "But I've made commitments and I can't back out!" Those thoughts are completely understandable, but what will your college application look like when your stress balloon pops? Or when you are so overwhelmed that you can't do any of these activities anymore? It doesn't have to be all or nothing. Try this:

Take some time to think about finding a balance in your schedule. Try answering these questions:

Are there any of these activities that I can drop?

_____

_____

Which of these activities do I like the least?

_____

_____

Which of these activities is the most important to me?

_____

_____

Are there any activities I can put off until my schedule is less hectic (like doing volunteer work only in the summer)?

_____

_____

Can I talk to my coaches, teachers, and leaders about cutting back my hours of commitment?

_____

_____

Okay, so now are you thinking, "But, if I can't handle it all, then I'm a failure!" or "My teachers/coaches/parents will be disappointed in me that I can't keep up!" These thoughts are your anxious alter ego really just being a jerk. You are seeing this situation through a negative and unrealistic filter. In reality, balancing all the things in your life is normal and healthy—it's a skill you'll need forever! All of the adults you know have had to do the exact same thing: find a way to cut back or prioritize their responsibilities when they are overwhelmed. It isn't failure; it's being responsible and finding helpful solutions. Take another look at the Shake Off Old Beliefs exercise (page 53) to help you reframe any unrealistic beliefs you may be having.

Q: I'm turning 16 soon, and I really don't want to do driver's ed. I just can't do it and don't know why. My parents don't mind driving me around, so why should I even bother?

A: *Your parents aren't in the driver's seat, anxiety is! Anxiety is keeping you from reaching this important milestone in your life. Probably without you realizing it, your mind is creating some amazing action-packed films with car crashes, speeding frenzies, and police chases! But real life is not* The Fast and the Furious 5! *Remember the* Fake News *exercise (page 47)? The scenarios you may picture are just creative thoughts and images from media—it's dramatization, and it's not real. Try to combat this with* Keeping It Real *(page 45). What is realistically going to happen? Take a moment to write down what is most likely to happen during the process of driver's ed and getting your driver's license.*

From my experience and that of many teens I've worked with, I can say that it actually goes something like this:

You will suffer through hours of boring class material. You'll take a super-easy written test. You'll spend hours slowly and gradually learning new driving skills; some will be easy, and some will be kind of challenging. You'll practice until you feel ready. You'll deal with your parents' backseat driving and irritating comments. Then you will take a practice driving test and learn if there is anything else you need to practice. When you are ready, you'll take the real driving test. You'll most likely pass, but if you don't pass, it's okay, you can retake it as many times as you need to. Failing the test doesn't reflect badly on you; it could have been that you were nervous so you forgot to make a complete stop at the stop sign. It just means you have a few skills to work on so you can be sure you're safe behind the wheel.

In reality, this is something you can handle and are totally capable of dealing with. By looking at what is REALLY likely to happen, it sounds far less scary and just something you get through for the prize at the end: independent driving, which can actually be fun! Don't let the anticipation of something new send your mind spinning into horror film mode. Reel it back in, and focus on what's more likely.

Q: **I can't talk to anyone about what I'm feeling. I feel totally alone. No one understands what it's like to have anxiety.**

A: *Anxiety is a little different for everyone who experiences it, so it's true that no one knows* exactly *what your experience is like. But anxiety is a human emotion that everyone is capable of feeling and has probably experienced to some degree. Teens are especially likely to know what anxiety feels like. And although anxiety feels overwhelming and can be difficult to talk about, you are definitely not alone. Think of it like this:*

* **What Would You Say?** (page 63) Imagine your friend was feeling like you do now, alone and too scared to talk about it. Would you want them to open up to you? What would you say to them? How do you think they would feel once they realized you understood where they were coming from?

* Part of friendship is being supportive of one another. Let a trusted friend hear about your experience and see if they can do what friends do best—offer support or a distraction, make you laugh, or maybe even tell you they are feeling the exact same way.

* If you're not sure if you need extra support or even who you can talk to, take a look at **How to Get Help** (page 22). Remember, there are lots of people on your team who are ready and willing to help you kick this anxiety thing!

Q: What about all these new viruses making people sick? Is a big earthquake coming? Tornadoes? Tsunamis? Nuclear war? AHHHHH!!!! The end is near, I know it! And I worry about all of it!

A: *Whoa, hold your horses! Your anxious alter ego sure does like to imagine that the end of the world is near, but any one of these apocalyptic scenarios is highly unlikely, let alone all of them! Here are some ways to save humanity and your sanity:*

1. One of anxiety's favorite tricks is to use the Fake News (page 47) tactic. It gets you thinking that you are in immediate and real danger. So anxiety creates these fantastic scenarios and images that will have you mentally building a doomsday bunker in your basement that's full of canned food and biohazard masks. But here's the thing: You are not in real danger. These are just thoughts that your anxious mind created. Sure, you may hear about disasters on the real news, but even that news is often dramatized for ratings and to grab your attention.

2. To combat the fake news freak-out, you need to redirect your thoughts. Sure, hazardous weather happens, and people catch viruses, but these rarely occur at disastrous levels. Use the Keeping It Real exercise (page 45) to reframe thoughts about these situations more realistically. "I don't live where tornadoes occur. The chances of me getting harmed in one of these situations is extremely small." Problem-solving can also make you feel more in control. You can say something like, "If hazardous weather occurs, I have a safety plan"—like going to an interior closet for a tornado or standing in a door frame for an earthquake. Or, "If I did catch a virus, I could go to my doctor for medicine. And it is highly unlikely that I would catch something that's not treatable!"

3. If all else fails, take these amazingly creative thoughts and write them down as a movie script or a short story. Go crazy with it—let your imagination flow, and, who knows, maybe you'll write the most epic disaster movie ever!

Q: I'm having a hard time keeping up in chemistry. It's so hard, and the teacher moves through the information so fast! I don't want her to know that I can't keep up, though. She'll think I'm stupid.

A: *We all want our teachers to be impressed by us. Surely you want them to see that you are working hard and getting good grades. But, no one can be a rock star at every single subject. Some classes are more challenging than others, and that's normal! If you're thinking, "It's embarrassing to ask my teacher for help. She'll think I'm stupid," stop for a moment. Does something seem off about that statement? Does this sound realistic? Do teachers hate helping kids? Do they want you to struggle or feel embarrassed and stupid? No, I didn't think so either. Give this a shot instead:*

1. Take another look at the Gray Thoughts exercise (page 43) to help you come up with different outcomes for talking to a teacher about their class. Consider these thoughts:

    Teachers typically want to help students who care and want to improve.

    My teacher may be able to help me find solutions to study better and improve my grades.

    My teacher can help me understand a concept better and will be happy to help me learn.

    Even if I continue to have a difficult time in this subject, at least my teacher will know that I am putting in the effort to improve. They'll see that I am a hardworking student, and they will want to help me succeed.

2. One of the best ways to challenge anxious thoughts like this is to avoid avoidance! By avoiding talking to your teacher, your brain will continue to think these thoughts are true. So try the Avoid Avoidance 1: A Little Science Experiment (page 87) strategy. Try talking to your teacher about the difficulty of their class and your hope that they will help you learn the material. See what happens! The worst thing that can happen is that they turn out to be a terrible teacher and don't offer help. In that case, they should be embarrassed, not you! But most likely they will offer some guidance and see you as the great student that you are.

Q: I took a test last week, and even though I studied and felt prepared, when the teacher placed the test in front of me, my mind went blank! I completely froze. I eventually remembered one or two things, but I got so anxious that I couldn't focus.

A: *Test anxiety is the worst! The answers are right there in your mind, but it's like they are just outside of your reach. Then you start to panic even more, and the answers get further and further away from you! Panicking during a test only makes it harder to get the information out of your memory. When this happens, it's okay; you can stop the panic from hijacking your brain and still ace the test. Try these strategies:*

1. As soon as you feel this anxiety creeping in on you, stop what you are doing. Put your pen down. Flip the test over to the back side or a blank page. I know the clock is running, but taking the time to get your mind and body right will help you—it's really worth the time. To learn more, visit the **Breathe!** exercise (page 75).

2. Flip the test back over. Skip around the test and try to find the questions you know the answers to. This will help you build your confidence back up. It's okay if you are skipping a lot. Just try to find ones that you know. As you complete the ones you know, you will start to feel more and more relaxed. As you relax, your mind will start to open up and more information that you studied will come forward. The ones that you skipped at first, you may be able to answer later on.

3. Get yourself psyched up, not psyched out. Give yourself a pep talk. Remind yourself that you studied hard. You just need to take this test without judging yourself. If the worst-case scenario happens and you can't answer the questions, you'll talk to the teacher and figure out some options. This test will not define your entire life. It's just one test. Do what you can.

4. Now, if none of this works, take your blank test to the teacher and tell her you are having high anxiety and need to talk to her about your options. I know that sounds like a horrible last resort, but it actually happens a lot, and your teacher should be able to make a plan with you.

Q: I was bullied in middle school, and all my friends abandoned me. I'm in high school now and have a group of friends who are nice, but I still have trouble trusting them. I get worried that they will also turn on me. I tend to turn down invites to hang out with them because I'm afraid they will do the same thing to me as my middle school friends did.

A: *Middle school is the worst. It can be so hard to have friendships that turn out to be phony or full of jealousy and competition. After such a bad experience, you may be thinking that you can protect yourself from getting hurt again if you keep your distance from your current friends. Keeping your distance and isolating yourself in middle school was probably helpful. It kept you safe from the bullying and from getting hurt even more by your jerky former "friends." Keeping your distance was the right call at that time. But now you are in a different school with different people, and you're all a bit more mature. The bullying is less prevalent, and people tend to be a bit more chill. So if the environment and people are all different, do you think you should still be doing the same things to your peers (keeping them at a distance), or is it safe to give your new friends the benefit of the doubt?*

If you think you should still be doing things the same way, there may be some Thinking Errors (page 30) occurring in this line of logic. Can you spot any? You may be *Overgeneralizing.* Overgeneralizing is when you use one bad experience to describe all experiences. The bullying in middle school sucked and was really hard, but it was only your middle school experience. It was one point in your life, and thankfully you are out of there. It's over! It would be an error to use that one point in your life to define everything that comes after. The bullying is no longer happening. You have more solid friends now. And you have probably learned a lot about what friendships should and should not be—so you have what it takes to be an awesome friend. Try to take steps to begin to trust others so you can enjoy the benefits of healthy friendships—a skill you'll want for life!

Try Avoiding Avoidance 1: a Little Science Experiment (page 87). Try applying this strategy to your current friendships. Here's an example of how this might play out:

Example Situation: Worried about spending time with friends because they will reject me	
HYPOTHESIS What do you expect or predict will happen?	I will let my guard down, and everyone in my group will turn against me and start bullying me.
EMOTION How do you feel? How strongly do you feel this will happen (0–100%)?	Anxious Sad Self-conscious 95% certain it will happen
EXPERIMENT How could you test this prediction? What can you do if the thing you are worried about happens?	I could start spending more time with my friends, little by little. Maybe I'll accept one invitation this weekend and see how it goes. If that goes well, then next weekend I could do more with my friends. If that goes well, then maybe I could invite some of them over to my house. If they start to be mean or bully me, I could use some assertiveness skills to stand up for myself.
OUTCOME What happened? Was your prediction true?	I spent Saturday with two of my friends. We hung out at their pool and had a lot of fun. I tried talking a bit more and being myself around them. They seemed to think I was nice and funny, and we made plans to hang out again. My prediction was not true—nobody tried to bully me or turn against me.
LEARNING What did you learn? What do you think will happen next time? How do you feel now?	We all seemed to get a bit closer when I acted like myself. They did not reject me or make fun of me. It felt good to finally be me and have fun. Next time, I'll try to open up a little bit more and see how that goes. I feel more confident in my friendships.

Q: My parents were in a car accident a couple of months ago. They were okay, but ever since then I can't stop worrying about them when they leave the house. I keep thinking they will be in another car accident and get hurt or die. When they leave the house, I think about them nonstop and have to call or text them like every 30 minutes to make sure they are okay.

A: *Car accidents can seem really scary, and they sure can trigger our flight-or-fight mode (page 14). It's normal to be a bit anxious and cautious after something like this happens. But we don't want our normal period of anxious adjustment to turn into avoidance and overwhelming fear. This might be a really good time to try the* Thoughts on Trial *exercise (page 35) to test the worry. Here's an example:*

Anxious Thought: "My parents will die in a car accident."	
EVIDENCE FOR **(THOUGHT IS REALISTIC)**	**EVIDENCE AGAINST** **(THOUGHT IS NOT REALISTIC)**
My parents were recently in a car accident. Car accidents happen all the time. I know lots of people who have had car accidents.	Car accidents happen frequently, but they usually result only in damage to the car itself. My parents were not hurt in the car accident. This is the first accident my parents have had in 12 years. All the people I know who have had car accidents had only minor injuries. No one has been seriously hurt. My parents are really good drivers; they are cautious, which prevents accidents. Cars are pretty safe these days, with all kinds of safety features, like air bags, sensors, and cameras, and some even have automatic braking to stop people from bumping into each other. And lives are saved because today most people wear their seatbelts. A Google search shows that the odds of dying in a car crash are 0.9 percent! That is almost as likely as dying from falling down, which is 0.8 percent. And I'm not worried when my parents are walking around. Neither are very likely!

Verdict: Anxious Thought Not Realistic

More Realistic Thought: My parents are safe drivers with a safe car. It is very unlikely that they will be in an accident, but if they are in an accident, they are going to be okay.

Q: I just got my first job! Now I can begin saving for a car! I am excited, but I am also getting pretty anxious as my first day gets closer. What if I make a mistake? What if my boss thinks I'm terrible and regrets hiring me? What if I get fired?!

A: *First things first: What an accomplishment! New opportunities like a first job are exciting, but they also tend to come with a big learning curve. This means you may make mistakes at first. And thoughts like "What if I make a mistake?" imply that mistakes are not okay. Let's face reality: You will probably make many mistakes. You've never done this job before, and the person who hires you knows that. Mistakes are expected as you learn the ins and outs of your new job. Look over the* Go Ahead, Make a Mistake! *exercise (page 57). Take a minute to consider the following:*

* When you make a mistake, what are some things you can do about it?

* When you make a mistake, does rumination and anxiety help you in any way?

* When others make a mistake, do you assume they will be fired?

Instead of letting anxiety make you feel terrible and incapable and worried that you will get fired, when you make a mistake, try this instead:

1. Own your mistake. Acknowledge that it happened and that it's okay. Say to yourself or your boss, "I made a mistake. How can I fix it or do this differently next time?"

2. Problem-solve. Learn from this situation, and use your creativity to determine a way to do it differently next time. If you aren't sure how, ask your colleagues or boss to help you learn how. Also, sneak a peek at the Rumination Illumination exercise (page 60)!

3. Be confident. Making a mistake should not steal your confidence. Try to remain calm and confident while you find solutions. Show off how awesome you are by recovering from mistakes quickly and being a confident problem solver.

4. Be appreciative. You don't have to do it alone. Ask others to help you learn and figure out solutions. Then let them know that you appreciate their help! Most bosses appreciate employees who ask lots of questions and show that they are eager to learn.

One Last Thing . . . You Got This!

The life of a teenager is incredibly challenging, and it sometimes seems like adults have forgotten what it's like to have so much demanded of you. You have so much you want to be, do, and become, and there are many people who also expect A LOT from you. It's stressful. It can be scary. It is often overwhelming. Having anxiety in response to all of this is normal.

The most important part of coping with anxiety is to believe in yourself and trust that **YOU ARE CAPABLE**. With the mind-set that you can do this, and the practice you get by doing the exercises in this book, you will become more and more skilled at keeping anxiety at a level that helps you rather than holds you back. A little anxiety can help you achieve things, so take that "just right" amount of anxiety and use it to your benefit!

A few tips to remember:

* **Ask for help.** When anxiety becomes "too much," get help from someone you trust, and lend a helping hand to those who are also feeling overwhelmed (see page 22). Helping others and showing them the skills you now have can strengthen this knowledge in your own mind while also building your confidence.

* **Practice.** Anxiety management is about learning new skills and habits. And just like with learning anything new (a new language, a new sport, a new instrument, etc.) it takes practice and repetition. Practice these skills even when you aren't feeling anxious—that way, when anxiety creeps in, your body and mind will know exactly what to do.

* **Be patient.** If a skill doesn't work for you the first time, that's okay. Keep at it and give it a real chance. Some skills take a few tries before you finally see results. If after you have given it a shot, it still isn't working for you, that's okay, too. Ditch it and try another one.

* **Be creative.** Harness your imagination to help you, rather than letting anxiety use it against you. This book has lots of ideas for how to beat anxiety, but you have a creative mind and can take these ideas or others and make them your own. If you have a way that you think will help you, use it!

* **Make time.** In the long run, making time to practice these skills and using them every day will be oh so worth it! Research shows that when anxiety is managed, grades go up, performance improves, relationships improve, and confidence skyrockets. Making time for yourself and taking care of your emotions is just as important as studying for that test or practicing for the next big game.

* **Stay cool.** You are capable, you are resilient, you are strong, and—most of all—you've got this! The more you continue working to stay calm and realistic in the face of life's challenges, the less frequently you will encounter anxiety. And the closer you will come to bidding farewell to a fake friend who's overstayed their welcome—goodbye anxious alter ego. There's a new person in charge from here on out—hello cool and confident YOU!

RESOURCES FOR TEENS

Anxiety Apps

AnxietyHelper
Companion
Pacifica
SAM

Websites

Anxiety in Teens, AnxietyInTeens.org

BODY SCAN/PROGRESSIVE MUSCLE RELAXATION

Website offering written scripts and audio recordings of various body scans and meditations:
"Free Guided Meditations," UCLA Health, UCLAHealth.org/marc /mindful-meditations

EIGHT-MINUTE BODY SCAN

YouTube Channel: Stop, Breathe & Think
Title: Body Scan Meditation (Tame Anxiety)
Link: YouTube.com/watch?v=QS2yDmWk0vs

LEARNING ABOUT YOUR BRAIN

This Ted Talk explains important information about your brain and emotions:
YouTube Channel: TEDx Talks
Title: Mindfulness and Neural Integration: Daniel Siegel, MD at TEDxStudioCityED
Link: YouTu.be/LiyaSr5aeho

Why Be Mindful?:
YouTube Channel: TED
Title: All It Takes Is 10 Mindful Minutes, Andy Puddicombe
Link: YouTube.com/watch?v=qzR62JJCMBQ

Six-Minute Mindful Moment:
YouTube Channel: Stop, Breathe & Think
Title: Relax, Ground, and Clear Meditation (Relieve Stress)
Link: YouTube.com/watch?v=zoCfRlKg3nM

Three-Minute Observing Thoughts:
YouTube Channel: Fablefy—The Whole Child
Title: Observing Your Thoughts—Mindfulness Meditation for Teens and Adults
Link: YouTube.com/watch?v=wJQeq4yqlbQ

Meditation Apps

Aura
Headspace
SimplyBeing

Sociability and Self-Confidence

Living in A Shell:
YouTube Channel: zefrank1
Title: If You Are in a Shell . . .
Link: YouTube.com/watch?v=elILetNPyr4&list=PL_cavQCHqf1LlBFADzx8GSXA8V0BCp1iO

Book: *The Teen's Guide to World Domination: Advice on Life, Liberty, and the Pursuit of Awesomeness,* by Josh Shipp

Just for Fun

Book: *What If? Serious Scientific Answers to Absurd Hypothetical Questions,* by Randall Munroe

RESOURCES FOR PARENTS

Books

Brainstorm: The Power and Purpose of the Teenage Brain, by Daniel Siegel, MD

Glow Kids: How Screen Addiction Is Hijacking Our Kids—and How to Break the Trance, by Nicholas Kardaras, PhD

Mindfulness for Beginners: Reclaiming the Present Moment—and Your Life, by Jon Kabat-Zinn

The Teenage Brain: A Neuroscientist's Survival Guide to Raising Adolescents and Young Adults, by Frances Jensen, MD, with Amy Nutt

The Yes Brain: How to Cultivate Courage, Curiosity, and Resilience in Your Child, by Daniel Siegel, PhD, and Tina Bryson, PhD

Websites/Podcasts

Anxiety and Depression Association of America (ADAA), "Podcasts About Children and Teens"
ADAA.org/living-with-anxiety/children/podcasts-children-teens

AT Parenting Survival
AnxiousToddlers.com

Erin Leyba, PhD, "25 Simple Self-Care Tools for Parents," *Psychology Today*, August 18, 2017
PsychologyToday.com/us/blog/joyful-parenting/201708/25-simple-self-care-tools-parents

Lynn Lyons, "Teen Anxiety Podcast: How Parents and Teens Can Challenge Anxiety Together"
LynnLyonsnh.com/parents-teens-challenge-anxiety-together

Susan Newman, PhD, "7 Ways to Cope with Anxiety About Your Teen," *Psychology Today*, July 11, 2018
PsychologyToday.com/us/blog/singletons/201807/7-ways-cope-anxiety-about-your-teen

REFERENCES

American Psychiatric Association. *Diagnostic and Statistical Manual of Mental Disorders: Diagnostic and Statistical Manual of Mental Disorders.* 5th ed. Arlington, VA: American Psychiatric Association, 2013.

Kessler, Ronald C., Ayelet M. Ruscio, Katherine Shear, and Hans-Ulrich Wittchen. "Epidemiology of Anxiety Disorders." *Current Topics in Behavioral Neurosciences* 2, no. 2 (January 2010): 21–35. doi:10.1007/7854_2009_9.

Kessler, Ronald C., Maria Petukhova, Nancy A. Sampson, Alan M. Zaslavsky, and Hans-Ulrich Wittchen. "Twelve-Month and Lifetime Prevalence and Lifetime Morbid Risk of Anxiety and Mood Disorders in the United States." *International Journal of Methods in Psychiatric Research* 21, no. 3 (September 2012): 169–84. doi:10.1002/mpr.1359.

King, Neville J., Elenora A. Gullone, and Thomas H. Ollendick. "Etiology of Childhood Phobias: Current Status of Rachman's Three Pathways Theory." *Behaviour Research and Therapy* 36, no. 3 (March 1998): 297–309. doi:10.1016/S0005-7967(01)00051-1.

LeBeau, Richard T., Daniel Glenn, Betty Liao, Hans-Ulrich Wittchen, Katja Beesdo-Baum, Thomas Ollendick, and Michelle G. Craske. "Specific Phobia: A Review of DSM-IV Specific Phobia and Proposals for DSM-V." *Depression and Anxiety* 27, no. 2 (February 2010): 148–67. doi:10.1002/da.20655.

Merikangas, Kathleen R., Jian-ping He, Marcy Burstein, Sonja A. Swanson, Shelli Avenevoli, Lihong Cui, Corina Banjet, Katholiki Georgiades, and Joel Swendsen. "Lifetime Prevalence of Mental Disorders in US Adolescents: Results from the National Comorbidity Study-Adolescent Supplement (NCS-A)." *Journal of the American Academy of Child and Adolescent Psychiatry* 49, no. 10 (October 2010): 980–89. doi:10.1016/j.jaac.2010.05.017.

National Institute of Mental Health (NIMH). "Prevalence of Any Anxiety Disorder Among Adolescents." Last modified November 2017. Accessed March 27, 2019. https://www.nimh.nih.gov/health/statistics/any-anxiety-disorder.shtml#part_155096.

National Sleep Foundation (NSF). *Adolescent Sleep Needs and Patterns: Research Report and Resource Guide.* Accessed March 27, 2019. https://www.sleepfoundation.org/sites/default/files/2019-02/sleep_and_teens_report1.pdf.

Rapee, Ronald M., Ann D. Wignall, Jennifer L. Hudson, and Carolyn A. Schniering. *Treating Anxious Children and Adolescents: An Evidence-Based Approach.* Oakland, CA: New Harbinger Publications, 2000.

Stinson, Frederick S., Deborah A. Dawson, S. Patricia Chou, Sharon Smith, Rise B. Goldstein, W. June Ruan, and Bridget F. Grant. "The Epidemiology of DSM-IV Specific Phobia in the USA: Results from the National Epidemiologic Survey on Alcohol and Related Conditions." *Psychological Medicine* 37, no. 7 (July 2007): 1047–59. doi:10.1017/S0033291707000086.

INDEX

ABOUT THE AUTHOR

Dr. Tabatha Chansard is a licensed clinical psychologist who specializes in cognitive behavioral therapy for a variety of emotional and behavioral difficulties. She treats childhood disorders and is passionate about her work with children, adolescents, and young adults.

Dr. Chansard received her doctoral degree in clinical psychology from the APA-accredited program at the University of Texas Southwestern Medical Center. During her training, she served as chief resident and worked with children, adolescents, and adults in a variety of clinical and medical settings. In her postdoctoral fellowship she further specialized in the treatment of anxiety disorders.

Dr. Chansard resides in Dallas with her husband and baby girl. She enjoys binge-watching a good Netflix series, basking in the warm Texas sun, and spending quality time with friends and family.

Dr. Chansard offers individual therapy and parent consultations in her Dallas community, with the goal of improving parent-child relationships and teaching universal skills for managing everyday emotions. She seeks to work empathetically and collaboratively with patients, their families, and patient support systems to provide comprehensive care to reduce distress, increase self-awareness, and promote emotional wellness.